Contents

Introduction

═══════════ ◨ ═══════════

Everyone loves stir-fries! Why? Because they are easy, quick, and versatile. They are perfect for dinner on a hectic work-day, as they can be cooked up in a flash. Many grocery stores now sell meat that has been already cut up for stir-fries, as well as pre-cut vegetables, making stir-fries even faster. And, they are also a great way to use up leftover vegetables, meat, chicken, or seafood—even pasta!

We have gathered the best stir-fries recipes here, ones that showcase their ease and diversity. If you'd like a meat stir-fry, you can choose from classics such as Sweet and Sour Beef, or try more unusual dishes such as Beef with Bow-tie Pasta or Italian Sausage and Vegetables.

Looking for chicken stir-fries? Then Creamy Spinach and Chicken Dinner, Wings with Black Beans or Lemon Chicken will fill the bill. And you will also enjoy our fish and seafood stir-fries—Halibut with Salted Black Beans, Stir-fried Garlic Shrimp or Lobster with Chinese Vegetables are just a few of your delectable choices.

New ways to serve vegetables are always welcome, especially when cooking for children. Stir-fries make eating vegetables easy and delicious, with recipes such as Lemon-Pepper Vegetables, Green Bean Stir-fry with Hoisin Sauce and Gingered Spinach.

We have also included a helpful glossary that explains the ingredients used in stir-fries, as well as information on stir-frying techniques and the various kinds of woks. Tips throughout will help you cut up food for stir-fries like an expert, and select and store your stir-fry ingredients.

With so many delicious stir-fries to choose from, we think you'll find this one of the most useful cookbooks in your kitchen!

THE BETTY CROCKER EDITORS

Stir-fry Magic

STIR-FRYING BASICS

Stir-frying originally was a Chinese method of cooking food quickly in a small amount of oil over high heat. When meat and vegetables are quickly tossed in hot oil, the meat remains tender and juicy and the vegetables crisp. Today, we enjoy stir-fries that reflect cuisines other than Chinese.

It is important to measure and prepare all ingredients before beginning to stir-fry. Just read the recipe completely before beginning. Assemble ingredients on a tray in the order in which they will be used. Place serving dishes near the range so that stir-fried food can be served immediately.

Always begin with a clean, dry wok or skillet. Before adding oil, heat the wok or skillet over high heat until a few drops of water sprinkled in it sizzle and evaporate. Use only 2 or 3 drops of water to test temperature; any remaining water in the wok will cause oil to splatter when it is added. If food sticks to the wok or moisture seeps from the meat and vegetables, either the wok is not sufficiently hot or too much food is being cooked at one time. If any food should stick, wash and dry the wok between steps as you cook.

Vegetable and peanut oil are used for stir-frying because they tolerate high heat. Margarine and butter are not used because they burn easily.

Use a spatula with a firm base, bringing it down the side of the wok and across the bottom to turn food over. Stir quickly, keeping food moving.

Stir-fried food is done when it changes in color; thinly sliced pork and chicken turn white and beef is no longer red. Vegetables become brighter in color while remaining crisp.

ALL ABOUT WOKS

This round-bottomed Chinese cooking vessel was designed for stir-frying in order to shorten cooking time and save fuel. While woks are made in sizes from 10 to 20 inches in diameter, the most versatile is 14 or 16 inches in diameter. The metal ringstand is to hold the round-bottomed wok securely on the surface of the range during cooking and can be used for safety.

The traditional bowl-shaped Chinese wok is made from heavy-gauge rolled carbon steel, which heats quickly and conducts heat evenly.

However, woks made of carbon steel require some special care and thorough drying after each use to prevent rusting. To season a new wok, wash with hot sudsy water; dry on the range over medium heat. Rub about 2 teaspoons of vegetable oil evenly over the inside of the wok with a soft cloth. Repeat the process if food begins to stick.

Aluminum and stainless steel woks do not conduct heat as evenly as carbon steel. However, since they do not rust, they are a good choice for steaming foods. They require no seasoning and are easier to care for.

Electric woks, some with nonstick cooking surfaces, are convenient for cooking at the table. Follow manufacturer's directions for their care and use. Most stir-fries also work well in a skillet—follow the directions given in the recipe.

GLOSSARY OF INGREDIENTS

Baby Corn: Light yellow, miniature ears of corn, 1½ to 2 inches long. Tender and juicy. Sold canned in water.

Bamboo Shoots: Young, tender, ivory-colored shoots from the tropical bamboo plant. Used as a vegetable. Sold whole, sliced or in chunks, water-packed in cans. The tender, pointed end of the shoot is used for stir-frying; the wide, less tender end is used for soups and stews or can be sliced very thin for stir-frying. Refrigerate bamboo shoots covered with cold water in a tightly-covered jar. Change the water daily.

Bean Curd (Bean cakes): Bland, smooth, custard-like mixture made from pureed soybeans. Fragile and requires very little cooking. Used as an inexpensive vegetable and a good source of protein. Refrigerate bean curd covered with water and tightly covered. Change water daily.

Bean Sprouts: Young, white sprouts of the mung bean, which have a crisp texture and delicate flavor. Sold fresh or canned. Should be rinsed in cold water to retain their crispness. Refrigerate covered with cold water in a covered container; use within four days.

Black Beans, Salted (Black fermented beans): Small black, fermented soybeans; strong, pungent and salty in flavor. Sold in jars, cans or plastic bags of various sizes. Soak beans in warm water for 15 minutes; rinse to remove salt and skins. (Although the skins do not affect the flavor of the beans, they make the finished dish less attractive.) Refrigerate tightly covered after opening. Brown bean sauce can be substituted.

Bok Choy (Chinese chard or white mustard cabbage): Resembles both chard and cabbage with crisp, white stalks and shiny, dark green leaves. Used cooked as a vegetable, in soups or in stir-fried dishes. Leaves can be separated from stalks and should be added to dishes last to prevent overcooking. Sold by the pound.

Brown Bean Sauce (Brown bean paste): A thick, salty sauce made from fermented yellow soybeans, flour and salt. Adds flavor to cooked meats or sauces. Sold whole or mashed in cans or jars. Whole beans should be mashed before using. Refrigerate tightly covered after opening. Dark soy sauce can be substituted.

Chile Paste (Chile paste with garlic, chile sauce or Sichuan paste): A hot, spicy sauce made from soybeans, hot peppers, salt, oil and garlic. Used in Sichuan cooking or as a condiment. Imported from Hong Kong and Taiwan and sold in jars or bottles. Refrigerate tightly covered after opening.

Chinese Cabbage (Napa, celery cabbage or sui choy): Solid, oblong heads of long, smooth stalks with pale green leaves.

Chinese Parsley (Cilantro or fresh coriander): A strongly flavored, aromatic herb with broad, flat, serrated leaves. Used as a garnish for hot and cold dishes. There is no substitute.

Five-spice Powder (Five spices, five-flavored powder, five-fragrance spice powder or five-fragrance powder): A mixture of five ground spices used to flavor food. It is slightly sweet and pungent. Star anise, cinnamon and cloves are usually three of the five spices used. Sold in jars or plastic bags. Store tightly covered in a dry place at room temperature.

Hoisin Sauce (Hoisen, hoison, haisein or Peking sauce): A thick, sweet reddish-brown sauce usually made from soybeans, vinegar, chiles, spices and garlic. Used in cooking and as a table condiment. Refrigerate tightly after opening. There is no substitute.

Mushrooms, Dried Black (Chinese dried mushrooms, dried Chinese mushrooms, black dried mushrooms, winter mushrooms): Brownish-black mushrooms with caps that vary in size from $\frac{1}{2}$ to 2 inches in diameter. Must be soaked in water until tender and washed before using. Store tightly covered at room temperature.

Mushrooms, Straw (Grass mushrooms): Tender, tall mushrooms with long leaflike caps. Sold canned or dried. Soak the dried mushrooms and wash many times in warm water before using. Refrigerate the canned mushrooms covered with water after opening.

Noodles, Cellophane (Bean threads, shining noodles, transparent noodles or vermicelli): Hard, clear white noodles made from mung peas. They become translucent, soft and gelatinous when they absorb liquid, and puffy and crisp when deep-fried. Sold in cellophane packages.

Oil: Vegetable, peanut or corn oil can be used for stir-frying and marinating foods. Peanut oil has a higher smoking point but is less economical than vegetable oil. Sesame oil, made from roasted white sesame seeds, has a nutlike flavor and is used sparingly for flavoring. Sesame oil purchased from Asian specialty stores is preferred to the paler, mild sesame oil sold in supermarkets. Refrigerate after opening to prevent rancidity.

Oyster Sauce: A thick, brown sauce made from oysters, salt, water and starch. Used as an ingredient or as a table condiment. Refrigerate tightly covered after opening. Half the amount of dark soy sauce can be substituted for the oyster sauce in recipes.

Pea Pods (Snow peas or Chinese peas): Tender, flat, green edible pea pods. Add crispness, color and a delicate flavor to Chinese dishes. Sold fresh or frozen.

Plum Sauce: A thick, piquant sauce made from plums, apricots, chiles, vinegar and spices. Used as a table condiment for duck and spareribs and as an ingredient in sauces for appetizers.

Soy Sauce: A salty brown sauce made from soybeans, wheat, yeast and salt. There are three specific types: light, dark and heavy. Light soy sauce, light in color and delicately flavored, is used in clear soups and in marinades. Dark soy is made from the same ingredients as light, with the addition of caramel for a richer, darker color. Both light and dark soy sauces can be used as table condiments. Heavy soy sauce is made with molasses and is thick and dark. It is used for color in dark sauces. Soy sauce is sold in bottles or cans and can be stored at room temperature.

Water Chestnuts: Crisp, white, delicately flavored bulb of an Asian marsh plant. Used as a vegetable for stir-frying and in soups and cold dishes. Available canned or fresh. If fresh, they must be washed and peeled before using.

HOW TO USE NUTRITION INFORMATION

Nutrition Information per serving for each recipe includes the amounts of calories. protein, carbohydrate, fat, cholesterol and sodium.

- If ingredient choices are given, the first listed ingredient is used in recipe nutrition information calculations.

- When ingredient ranges or more than one serving size is indicatd, the first weight or serving is used to calculate nutrition information.

- "If desired" ingredients and recipe variations are not included in nutrition information calculations.

MENUS

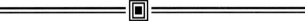

Work-Day Dinner
Beef with Pea Pods (page 12)
Rice
Pineapple Slices and Cookies
Tea

Company Fare
Sharp Cheddar Spread and Crackers
Lobster with Chinese Vegetables (page 77)
Sundaes
Wine or Seltzer

Kid-Pleasing Dinner
Grilled Hamburgers
Green Bean Stir-fry with Hoisin Sauce (page 79)
Brownies
Milk

Meatless Dinner
Stir-fried Bok Choy with Tofu (page 89)
Rice Stick Noodles
Cucumber and Tomato Skillet (page 83)
Carrot Cake
Fruit Juice

Hearty Winter Dinner
Stir-fried Pork and Pasta (page 29)
Spicy Zucchini (page 80)
Garlic Bread
Apple Crisp
Wine or Sparkling Water

Pleasing Poultry
Walnut Chicken (page 52)
Brown Rice
Triple Mushroom Stir-fry (page 87)
Frozen Yogurt or Sorbet
Coffee or Tea

Stir-fried Beef and Tomatoes (Recipe on page 14); Mandarin Beef (Recipe on page 17)

1
Meat

Beef and Broccoli with Garlic Sauce

White pepper is very attractive in this dish; but you can also use black pepper, if you like.

**1 pound beef boneless sirloin or round
   steak**
1 tablespoon vegetable oil
½ teaspoon salt
Dash of white pepper
1½ pounds broccoli
1 teaspoon cornstarch
1 teaspoon sesame oil
¼ cup chicken broth
2 tablespoons vegetable oil
1 tablespoon vegetable oil
1 tablespoon finely chopped garlic
1 teaspoon finely chopped gingerroot
2 tablespoons brown bean sauce
1 cup sliced canned bamboo shoots

Trim fat from beef steak; cut beef lengthwise into 2-inch strips. Cut strips crosswise into ⅛-inch slices. Toss beef, 1 tablespoon vegetable oil, the salt and white pepper in medium bowl. Cover and refrigerate 30 minutes.

Pare outer layer from broccoli stalks. Cut broccoli lengthwise into 1-inch stems; remove flowerets. Cut stems into 1-inch pieces. Place broccoli in boiling water; heat to boiling. Cover and cook 2 minutes; drain. Immediately rinse in cold water; drain. Mix cornstarch, sesame oil and broth.

Heat wok until very hot. Add 2 tablespoons vegetable oil; tilt wok to coat side. Add beef; stir-fry 2 minutes or until beef is brown. Remove beef from wok.

Heat wok until very hot. Add 1 tablespoon oil; tilt wok to coat side. Add garlic, gingerroot and bean sauce; stir-fry 30 seconds. Add bamboo shoots; stir-fry 1 minute. Stir in beef and broccoli. Stir in cornstarch mixture; cook and stir 15 seconds or until thickened.   **4 servings**

PER SERVING: Calories 350;   Protein 33 g; Carbohydrate 9 g; Fat 20 g; Cholesterol 75 mg; Sodium 910 mg

Beef with Pea Pods

2 pounds lean beef boneless round
   steak, ¾ to 1 inch thick
1 clove garlic, finely chopped
½ teaspoon salt
Dash of pepper
1 can (10½ ounces) condensed beef
   broth
2 tablespoons cornstarch
¼ cup water
1 tablespoon soy sauce
¼ teaspoon crushed gingerroot or ⅛ teaspoon ground ginger
1 package (7 ounces) frozen Chinese pea
   pods
4 cups hot cooked rice

Trim fat from beef steak; cut beef with grain into 2-inch strips. Cut strips diagonally across grain into ¼-inch slices. (For ease in cutting, partially freeze beef, about 2 hours.) Cook and stir beef and garlic in 10-inch nonstick skillet or wok over medium-high heat until beef is brown. Sprinkle with salt and pepper; stir in broth. Heat to boiling; reduce heat. Simmer uncovered until beef is tender, 10 to 15 minutes. (Add water if necessary.)

Mix cornstarch, water and soy sauce; stir into beef mixture. Cook until mixture thickens and boils, stirring constantly. Boil and stir 1 minute. (Gravy will be thin.) Stir in gingerroot and pea pods. Cook, stirring occasionally, until pea pods are crisp-tender, about 5 minutes. Serve over rice. **8 servings**

PER SERVING: Calories 285; Protein 28 g; Carbohydrate 30 g; Fat 5 g; Cholesterol 70 mg; Sodium 950 mg

Spicy Stir-fried Beef

1½ pounds beef boneless sirloin steak
1 tablespoon cornstarch
1 tablespoon vegetable oil
1 tablespoon soy sauce
1 teaspoon sugar
¼ teaspoon salt
¼ teaspoon pepper
1 tablespoon soy sauce
¼ to ½ teaspoon finely crushed dried
   red pepper
2 tablespoons vegetable oil
1 teaspoon finely chopped gingerroot
2 large cloves garlic, finely chopped
1 large green bell pepper, cut into
   ¼-inch strips
2 medium carrots, shredded (about 1
   cup)
1 can (8 ounces) bamboo shoots,
   drained
1 can (8 ounces) sliced water chestnuts
4 green onions (with tops), cut into
   2-inch pieces

Trim fat from beef steak. Cut beef into 2-inch strips. Cut strips into ⅛-inch slices. Stack slices and cut into thin strips. (For ease in cutting, partially freeze beef, about 2 hours.) Toss beef, cornstarch, 1 tablespoon oil, 1 tablespoon soy sauce, the sugar, salt and red pepper in glass or plastic bowl. Cover and refrigerate 30 minutes. Mix 1 tablespoon soy sauce and the red pepper; let stand at room temperature.

Heat 2 tablespoons oil in 12-inch skillet or wok over high heat until hot. Add beef mixture, gingerroot and garlic; cook and stir until beef is brown, about 5 minutes. Add bell pepper, carrots, bamboo shoots and water chestnuts; cook and stir 3 minutes. Add onions and red pepper mixture; cook and stir 1 minute.

6 servings

PER SERVING: Calories 265; Protein 30 g; Carbohydrate 12 g; Fat 11 g; Cholesterol 75 mg; Sodium 510 mg.

Spicy Beef with Cellophane Noodles

Cellophane noodles aren't traditional pasta, but translucent threads made from the starch of green mung beans.

1 package (3¾ ounces) cellophane
    noodles
6 ounces fresh Chinese pea pods*
2 tablespoons soy sauce
2 tablespoons rice wine vinegar
2 teaspoons grated gingerroot or ½ tea-
    spoon ground ginger
1 teaspoon cornstarch
2 teaspoons honey
½ teaspoon crushed red pepper
¼ teaspoon salt
1-pound lean beef boneless round steak
1 teaspoon sesame oil
2 cloves garlic, finely chopped
1 teaspoon sesame oil
1 cup thinly sliced carrots (about 2 large)
1 can (8 ounces) sliced water chestnuts,
    drained

Cover noodles with hot water. Let stand 10 minutes; drain. Remove strings from pea pods. Place pea pods in boiling water in 2-quart saucepan. Cover and cook 1 minute; drain. Immediately rinse with cold water; drain. Mix soy sauce, vinegar, gingerroot, cornstarch, honey, red pepper and salt; reserve.

Trim fat from beef steak. Cut beef with grain into 2-inch strips. Cut strips across grain into ⅛-inch slices. (For ease in cutting, partially freeze beef, about 1 hour.) Heat 1 teaspoon sesame oil in 10-inch nonstick skillet over medium-high heat. Add beef and garlic; stir-fry about 3 minutes or until beef is no longer pink. Remove beef from skillet. Add 1 teaspoon sesame oil to skillet. Add

*1 package (6 ounces) frozen Chinese pea pods, thawed and drained, can be substituted for the fresh pea pods. Do not remove strings or cook.

carrots and water chestnuts; stir-fry about 1 minute or until carrots are crisp-tender. Stir in beef mixture and cornstarch mixture; cook and stir about 30 seconds or until thickened. Stir in pea pods; cook and stir 30 seconds. Serve over noodles. **4 servings**

PER SERVING: Calories 320; Protein 34 g; Carbohydrate 25 g; Fat 8 g; Cholesterol 85 mg; Sodium 740 mg

Garlicky Beef with Peppers

1 pound lean beef boneless round steak,
    about ½ inch thick
1 tablespoon reduced-calorie margarine
¼ cup chopped onion (about 1 small)
4 cloves garlic, finely chopped
1 to 2 tablespoons chopped fresh or 1 to
    2 teaspoons dried thyme leaves
¼ teaspoon salt
¼ teaspoon pepper
2 bell peppers, cut into ¼-inch strips
¼ cup dry red wine or beef broth
2 tablespoons cornstarch
1 cup cold beef broth
3 cups hot cooked rice

Trim fat from beef steak; cut beef with grain into 2-inch strips. Cut strips diagonally across grain into ¼-inch slices. (For ease in cutting, partially freeze beef, about 1½ hours.) Heat margarine in 10-inch nonstick skillet until melted. Add onion, garlic, thyme, salt and pepper; cook and stir over medium-high heat until onion is tender, about 3 minutes. Stir in beef and bell peppers; cook and stir until beef is no longer pink, about 4 minutes.

Stir in wine; reduce heat. Cover and simmer 5 minutes. Stir cornstarch into cold broth until dissolved; stir into beef mixture. Cook and stir over medium-high heat until thickened. Serve over rice. **6 servings**

PER SERVING: Calories 280; Protein 20 g; Carbohydrate 35 g; Fat 6 g; Cholesterol 50 mg; Sodium 540 mg

Stir-fried Beef and Tomatoes

1 pound beef boneless sirloin or round
   steak
1 teaspoon vegetable oil
1 teaspoon cornstarch
1 teaspoon salt
⅛ teaspoon white pepper
3 medium tomatoes
1 small white onion
2 green onions (with tops)
3 tablespoons salted black beans
2 tablespoons cornstarch
1 tablespoon sugar
2 tablespoons water
2 tablespoons vegetable oil
2 tablespoons vegetable oil
1 teaspoon finely chopped gingerroot
1 teaspoon finely chopped garlic
½ cup chicken broth

Trim fat from beef steak; cut beef lengthwise into 2-inch strips. Cut strips crosswise into ⅛-inch slices. Toss beef, 1 teaspoon vegetable oil, 1 teaspoon cornstarch, the salt and white pepper in medium bowl. Cover and refrigerate 30 minutes.

Cut each tomato into 8 wedges. Cut white onion into 1-inch squares. Cut green onions diagonally into 1-inch pieces. Place beans in small bowl; cover with warm water. Stir beans about 2 minutes to remove excess salt. Remove beans from water; drain well. Mix 2 tablespoons cornstarch, the sugar and water.

Heat wok until very hot. Add 2 tablespoons oil; tilt wok to coat side. Add beef; stir-fry 2 minutes or until beef is brown. Remove beef from wok.

Heat wok until very hot. Add 2 tablespoons oil; tilt wok to coat side. Add tomatoes, white onion, beans, gingerroot, and garlic; stir-fry 1 minute. Add broth; heat to boiling. Stir in cornstarch mixture; cook and stir 15 seconds or until thickened.

Add beef and green onions; stir 30 seconds or until beef is hot. **4 servings**

PER SERVING: Calories 365; Protein 30 g; Carbohydrate 16 g; Fat 20 g; Cholesterol 75 mg; Sodium 790 mg

Tips for Slicing and Shredding Meat

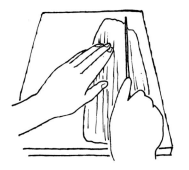

1. *Cut meat with the grain into long strips about 2 inches wide.*

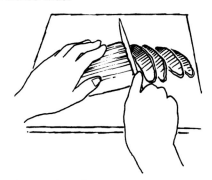

2. *Cut each strip across grain into 1/8-inch slices.*

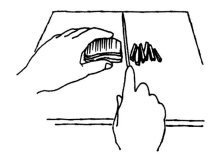

3. *To shred meat, stack slices and cut into thin strips.*

Stir-fried Beef with Green Beans

¾ pound beef flank or boneless sirloin
    steak
1 tablespoon vegetable oil
1 teaspoon cornstarch
1 teaspoon soy sauce
½ teaspoon salt
Dash of white pepper
1 pound green beans
2 green onions (with tops)
2 tablespoons cornstarch
2 tablespoons cold water
3 tablespoons vegetable oil
1 medium onion, thinly sliced
1 clove garlic, finely chopped
3 tablespoons vegetable oil
1 teaspoon salt
½ cup chicken broth
1 tablespoon dark soy sauce

Trim fat from beef; cut beef with grain into 2-inch strips. Cut strips across grain into ⅛-inch slices. Toss beef, 1 tablespoon oil, 1 teaspoon cornstarch, 1 teaspoon soy sauce, ½ teaspoon salt and the white pepper in glass or plastic bowl. Cover and refrigerate 20 minutes.

Remove ends from beans. Cut beans into 2-inch pieces. Cut green onions into 2-inch pieces. Mix 2 tablespoons cornstarch and the water.

Heat wok until 1 or 2 drops of water bubble and skitter when sprinkled in wok. Add 3 tablespoons oil; rotate wok to coat side. Add beef, onion and garlic; stir-fry until beef is brown, about 3 minutes. Remove beef mixture from wok.

Add 3 tablespoons oil to wok; rotate to coat side. Add beans and 1 teaspoon salt; stir-fry 2 minutes. Stir in broth; heat to boiling. Cover and cook 2 minutes. Stir in beef; heat to boiling. Stir in cornstarch mixture; cook and stir until thickened, about 15 seconds. Stir in green onions and 1 tablespoon dark soy sauce; heat to boiling. **5 servings**

PER SERVING: Calories 330; Protein 17 g; Carbohydrate 11 g; Fat 24 g; Cholesterol 40 mg; Sodium 1040 mg

Stir-fried Beef with Zucchini

1 pound beef flank or boneless sirloin
  steak
1 tablespoon vegetable oil
1 teaspoon cornstarch
1 teaspoon salt
1 teaspoon soy sauce
Dash of white pepper
1 pound zucchini
1 medium onion
1 tablespoon cornstarch
1 tablespoon cold water
3 tablespoons vegetable oil
1 teaspoon finely chopped garlic (about
  2 cloves)
3 tablespoons vegetable oil
1 tablespoon soy sauce
1 teaspoon salt
½ cup chicken broth or water

Trim fat from beef; cut beef with grain into 2-inch strips. Cut strips across grain into ⅛-inch slices. Toss beef, 1 tablespoon oil, 1 teaspoon cornstarch, 1 teaspoon salt, 1 teaspoon soy sauce and the white pepper in glass or plastic bowl. Cover and refrigerate 20 minutes.

Cut zucchini lengthwise into halves; cut each half diagonally into ¼-inch slices. Cut onion into halves. Place each half cut side down; cut into thin slices. Mix 1 tablespoon cornstarch and the water.

Heat wok until 1 or 2 drops of water bubble and skitter when sprinkled in wok. Add 3 tablespoons oil; rotate wok to coat side. Add beef and garlic; stir-fry until beef is brown, about 3 minutes. Remove beef from wok.

Add 3 tablespoons oil to wok; rotate to coat side. Add onion; stir-fry until tender, about 2 minutes. Add zucchini; stir-fry 1 minute. Stir in 1 tablespoon soy sauce and 1 teaspoon salt. Stir in broth; heat to boiling. Stir in beef; heat to boiling. Stir in cornstarch mixture; cook and stir until thickened, about 20 seconds.

5 servings

PER SERVING: Calories 350; Protein 21 g; Carbohydrate 8 g; Fat 26 g; Cholesterol 50 mg; Sodium 1250 mg

Mandarin Beef

Like all stir-fries, this is nice served over rice or noodles.

1 pound beef boneless sirloin or round steak
1 tablespoon vegetable oil
2 teaspoons cornstarch
1 teaspoon salt
1 teaspoon soy sauce
½ teaspoon sugar
¼ teaspoon white pepper
2 green onions (with tops)
1 large green bell pepper
¼ cup vegetable oil
1 teaspoon finely chopped gingerroot
1 teaspoon finely chopped garlic
¾ cup shredded carrot
1 to 2 teaspoons chile paste
1 tablespoon dark soy sauce

Trim fat from beef steak; cut beef lengthwise into 2-inch strips. Cut strips crosswise into ⅛-inch slices. Stack slices and cut lengthwise into thin strips. Toss beef, 1 tablespoon oil, the cornstarch, salt, 1 teaspoon soy sauce, the sugar and white pepper in medium glass or plastic bowl. Cover and refrigerate 30 minutes.

Cut green onions diagonally into 2-inch pieces. Cut bell pepper into ⅛-inch strips.

Heat wok until very hot. Add ¼ cup oil; tilt wok to coat side. Add beef, gingerroot and garlic; stir-fry 3 minutes or until beef is brown. Add bell pepper, carrot and chile paste; stir-fry 1 minute. Stir in green onions and 1 tablespoon dark soy sauce; stir-fry 30 seconds. **4 servings**

PER SERVING: Calories 345; Protein 29 g; Carbohydrate 8 g; Fat 22 g; Cholesterol 75 mg; Sodium 970 mg

Beef with Bow-tie Pasta

Fresh Parmesan cheese sprinkled on top of the dish adds a nice finishing touch. If you have a fine shredder, use that instead of a grater for a more elegant look.

1½ pounds beef boneless sirloin steak
3 cups 2-inch pieces asparagus (about 1 pound)
1 cup sliced onions (about 2 medium)
1½ cups beef broth
4 cups cooked farfalle (bow-tie-shape) pasta
1 cup tomato puree
3 tablespoons chopped fresh or 1 tablespoon dried basil leaves
3 tablespoons chopped sun-dried tomatoes (not oil-packed)
¼ teaspoon pepper
2 tablespoons freshly grated Parmesan cheese

Spray 12-inch skillet with nonstick cooking spray. Trim fat from beef steak. Cut beef into 2-inch strips. Cut strips crosswise into ⅛-inch slices. (For ease in cutting, partially freeze beef, about 1½ hours.) Heat skillet over medium heat until hot. Cook asparagus, onions and 1 cup of the broth 5 to 7 minutes, stirring occasionally, until liquid has evaporated. Remove from skillet.

Add beef to skillet; cook, stirring frequently, about 2 minutes or until beef is no longer pink. Return vegetables to skillet. Add remaining broth and ingredients except cheese; cook about 2 minutes, stirring frequently or until mixture is hot. Sprinkle with cheese. **6 servings**

PER SERVING: Calories 315; Protein 30 g; Carbohydrate 37 g; Fat 5 g; Cholesterol 55 mg; Sodium 400 mg

Stir-fried Orange Beef

Orange juice adds a fresh flavor to this hearty dish.

½ cup cold water
2 tablespoons cornstarch
2 tablespoons soy sauce
1 pound beef boneless sirloin steak
3 tablespoons vegetable oil
¼ teaspoon ground ginger
¼ teaspoon garlic powder
2 tablespoons vegetable oil
3 cups vegetable pieces (sliced mushrooms, broccoli flowerets, cauliflowerets, sliced carrots, celery, onion or bell pepper)
1 cup orange juice
2 cups hot cooked rice

Mix water, cornstarch and soy sauce; reserve. Trim fat from beef steak. Cut beef steak with grain into 2-inch strips. Cut strips across grain into ⅛-inch slices. (For ease in cutting, partially freeze beef, about 1½ hours.) Heat wok or 12-inch skillet until 1 or 2 drops of water bubble and skitter when sprinkled in wok. Add 3 tablespoons oil and rotate wok to coat side. Add beef, ginger and garlic powder. Stir-fry about 3 minutes or until beef is brown. Remove beef from wok.

Add 2 tablespoons oil to wok and rotate wok to coat side. Add vegetables. Stir-fry 1 minute. Stir in beef and orange juice; heat to boiling. Stir in cornstarch mixture. Cook and stir about 1 minute or until thickened. Serve with rice.

4 servings

PER SERVING: Calories 525; Protein 29 g; Carbohydrate 42 g; Fat 27 g; Cholesterol 70 mg; Sodium 970 mg

Sweet-and-Sour Beef

1 pound beef flank steak
3 tablespoons vegetable oil
1 medium onion, cut into 1-inch pieces
1 can (8 ounces) pineapple chunks in juice, undrained
¼ cup sugar
¼ cup white vinegar
1 tablespoon chicken bouillon granules
1 tablespoon soy sauce
1 tablespoon cornstarch
1 tablespoon cold water
1 medium green bell pepper, cut into 1-inch pieces
2 medium tomatoes, each cut into eighths

Trim fat from beef steak. Cut beef with grain into 2-inch strips. Cut strips across grain into ⅛-inch slices. (For ease in cutting, partially freeze beef, about 1½ hours.)

Heat oil in 12-inch skillet or wok over medium-high heat until hot. Add beef and onion; cook and stir until beef is brown, about 3 minutes. Stir in pineapple, sugar, vinegar, bouillon granules and soy sauce. Heat to boiling.

Mix cornstarch and cold water; stir into beef mixture. Cook and stir 1 minute. Stir in bell pepper and tomatoes; cook and stir 1 minute. Serve with hot cooked rice if desired.   **5 servings**

PER SERVING: Calories 325; Protein 21 g; Carbohydrate 26 g; Fat 15 g; Cholesterol 55 mg; Sodium 1020 mg

Oriental Beef with Rice Noodles

¾ **pound lean beef boneless round steak**
2 **tablespoons sake (rice wine), sherry or chicken broth**
1 **tablespoon finely chopped gingerroot or 1 teaspoon ground ginger**
2 **teaspoons vegetable oil**
½ **teaspoon salt**
1 **clove garlic, crushed**
4 **ounces rice noodles**
1 **teaspoon vegetable oil**
2 **cups thinly sliced bok choy with leaves (about 3 large stalks)**
½ **cup sliced green onions (with tops) (about 4 medium)**
1 **can (15 ounces) straw mushrooms, drained***
2 **tablespoons sake (rice wine), sherry or chicken broth**

Trim fat from beef steak. Cut beef diagonally into ¼-inch strips. Mix beef, 2 tablespoons sake, the gingerroot, 2 teaspoons oil, the salt and garlic in medium glass or plastic bowl. Cover and refrigerate 30 minutes.

Place rice noodles in large bowl. Cover with hot water. Let stand 10 minutes; drain well. Chop coarsely.

Heat 1 teaspoon oil in wok or 12-inch skillet until very hot. Add beef mixture; stir-fry about 5 minutes or until beef is done. Add rice noodles, bok choy, onions and mushrooms; stir-fry about 4 minutes or until box choy is crisp-tender. Sprinkle with 2 tablespoons sake.   **4 servings**

2 jars (4.5 ounces each) whole mushrooms, drained, can be substituted for the straw mushrooms.

PER SERVING: Calories 205; Protein 18 g; Carbohydrate 18 g; Fat 5 g; Cholesterol 40 mg; Sodium 380 mg

Pepper Steak

A family favorite!

1 pound beef flank or boneless sirloin
   steak
1 tablespoon vegetable oil
1 teaspoon cornstarch
1 teaspoon salt
1 teaspoon soy sauce
Dash of white pepper
3 small tomatoes
2 medium green bell peppers
1 medium onion
¼ cup chicken broth
2 tablespoons cornstarch
2 tablespoons dark soy sauce
1 teaspoon sugar
3 tablespoons vegetable oil
1 teaspoon finely chopped gingerroot
1 teaspoon finely chopped garlic
2 tablespoons vegetable oil
½ cup chicken broth

Trim fat from beef; cut beef with grain into 2-inch strips. Cut strips across grain into ⅛-inch slices. (For ease in cutting, partially freeze beef, about 1½ hours.) Toss beef, 1 tablespoon vegetable oil, 1 teaspoon cornstarch, the salt, I teaspoon soy sauce and the white pepper in glass bowl. Refrigerate 30 minutes.

Cut each tomato into 8 wedges. Cut bell peppers into 1-inch pieces. Cut onion into ¾-inch pieces. Mix ¼ cup broth, 2 tablespoons cornstarch, 2 tablespoons dark soy sauce and the sugar.

Heat wok until 2 drops of water bubble and skitter. Add 3 tablespoons oil; rotate to coat side. Add onion, gingerroot and garlic; stir-fry until garlic is light brown. Add beef; stir-fry until beef is brown, about 3 minutes. Remove beef from wok.

Add 2 tablespoons oil; rotate to coat side. Add tomatoes; stir-fry 30 seconds. Stir in ½ cup chicken broth; heat to boiling. Stir in cornstarch mixture; cook and stir until thickened. Add bell peppers and beef; stir-fry 30 seconds.

6 servings

MICROWAVE REHEAT DIRECTIONS: Prepare Pepper Steak as directed—except omit tomatoes and green peppers; cover and refrigerate no longer than 48 hours. To serve, prepare tomatoes and green peppers. Cover beef mixture tightly and microwave on microwaveproof platter on high power 5 minutes; stir in tomatoes and bell peppers. Cover and microwave until hot, about 4 minutes.

PER SERVING: Calories 285; Protein 18 g; Carbohydrate 10 g; Fat 19 g; Cholesterol 45 mg; Sodium 900 mg

Sesame Beef

1 pound beef boneless sirloin steak
2 tablespoons sugar
2 tablespoons vegetable oil
2 tablespoons soy sauce
¼ teaspoon pepper
3 green onions (with tops), finely
   chopped
2 cloves garlic, crushed
1 tablespoon sesame seed
1 tablespoon vegetable oil
3 cups hot cooked rice

Trim fat from beef steak; cut beef diagonally across grain into ⅛-inch slices. (For ease in cutting, partially freeze beef, about 1½ hours.) Mix sugar, 2 tablespoons oil, the soy sauce, pepper, onions and garlic in glass or plastic bowl; stir in beef until well coated. Cover and refrigerate 30 minutes.

Drain beef. Cook and stir sesame seed in 10-inch skillet over medium heat until golden brown; remove from skillet. Heat 1 tablespoon oil in same skillet until hot; add beef. Cook and stir beef in oil over medium-high heat until light brown, 3 to 4 minutes. Sprinkle with sesame seed. Serve over rice.   **5 servings**

PER SERVING: Calories 390; Protein 27 g; Carbohydrate 41 g; Fat 13 g; Cholesterol 60 mg; Sodium 930 mg

Selecting Meats

Beef
The color of the lean portions should be bright red. Vacuum-packaged beef has a darker, purplish-red color because the meat is not exposed to air; as this beef is exposed to the air, its color turns to the familiar bright red.

Veal
It should have a fine grain and be creamy pink in color. Any fat covering should be milky white.

Pork
The lean part of fresh pork should be grayish pink in color and fine grained in texture. For ham, the lean should be firm, fine grained, pink in color and free from excess moisture. The fat cover should be firm and white.

Lamb
Look for meat that is pinkish red and has a velvety texture. There is little marbling and only a thin layer of fat around the outside of the meat. The bones should be porous and reddish.

Shredded Veal with Ginger

Shredded Veal with Ginger

1 pound veal boneless steak
1 tablespoon cornstarch
½ teaspoon salt
⅛ teaspoon white pepper
6 green onions (with tops)
½ teaspoon cornstarch
½ teaspoon sugar
1 tablespoon chicken broth
1 teaspoon light soy sauce
2 tablespoons vegetable oil
1 tablespoon shredded gingerroot

Trim fat from veal steak; cut veal lengthwise into 2-inch strips. Cut strips crosswise into ⅛-inch slices. Stack slices; cut lengthwise into thin strips. (For ease in cutting, freeze veal partially, about 1½ hours.) Toss veal, 1 tablespoon cornstarch, the salt and white pepper in medium bowl. Cover and refrigerate 30 minutes.

Cut onions diagonally into 1-inch pieces. Mix ½ teaspoon cornstarch, the sugar, broth and soy sauce.

Heat wok until very hot. Add oil; tilt wok to coat side. Add veal and gingerroot; stir-fry 2 minutes or until veal turns white. Add green onions; stir-fry 10 seconds. Stir in cornstarch mixture; cook and stir 15 seconds or until thickened.

4 servings

PER SERVING: Calories 190; Protein 18 g; Carbohydrate 5 g; Fat 11 g; Cholesterol 75 mg; Sodium 430 mg

Mongolian Lamb

This lamb stir-fry is a lovely change of pace, a pleasant twist on beef and pork dishes.

2 pounds boneless leg of lamb
1 tablespoon cornstarch
1 tablespoon vegetable oil
2 teaspoons sugar
1 teaspoon salt
1 teaspoon white pepper
4 green onions (with tops)
3 tablespoons vegetable oil
1 teaspoon dried red pepper flakes
1 tablespoon brown bean sauce
2 teaspoons finely chopped garlic
1 teaspoon finely chopped gingerroot
2 teaspoons dark soy sauce

Trim fat from leg of lamb; cut lamb with grain into 2 × 1-inch strips. Cut strips across grain into ⅛-inch slices. (For ease in cutting, partially freeze lamb, about 2 hours.) Toss lamb, cornstarch, 1 tablespoon oil, the sugar, salt and white pepper in medium bowl. Cover and refrigerate 30 minutes. Cut green onions diagonally into 1-inch pieces.

Heat wok until very hot. Add 3 tablespoons oil; tilt wok to coat side. Add red pepper flakes, bean sauce, garlic and gingerroot; stir-fry 5 seconds. Add lamb; stir-fry 2 minutes or until brown. Add soy sauce and onions; stir-fry 30 seconds.

4 servings

PER SERVING: Calories 605; Protein 65 g; Carbohydrate 7 g; Fat 35 g; Cholesterol 210 mg; Sodium 900 mg

Gingered Pork with Nectarines

1 pound pork boneless shoulder or loin
1 tablespoon dry white wine
1 tablespoon soy sauce
1 teaspoon cornstarch
1 teaspoon sugar
3 tablespoons vegetable oil
1 teaspoon finely chopped gingerroot or
** 1 teaspoon ground ginger**
1 green bell pepper, cut into 1-inch
** pieces**
1 can (8 ounces) sliced water chestnuts,
** drained**
¼ cup cold water
2 tablespoons cornstarch
1 cup chicken broth
2 large nectarines, sliced*
½ cup salted nuts
Cooked Chinese noodles or rice

Cut pork with grain into 2-inch strips. Cut strips across grain into ⅛-inch slices. (For ease in cutting, partially freeze pork, about 1½ hours.) Toss pork, wine, soy sauce, 1 teaspoon cornstarch and the sugar in glass or plastic bowl. Cover and refrigerate 20 minutes.

Heat 12-inch skillet or wok until 1 or 2 drops of water bubble and skitter when sprinkled in skillet. Add oil; rotate skillet to coat bottom. Add pork and gingerroot; cook and stir until pork is no longer pink. Add bell pepper and water chestnuts; cook and stir 1 minute.

Mix cold water and 2 tablespoons cornstarch; stir broth and cornstarch mixture into pork mixture. Heat to boiling. Boil and stir 1 minute; stir in nectarines. Sprinkle with nuts. Serve with noodles. **4 servings**

1 can (16 ounces) sliced peaches, drained, can be substituted for the nectarines.

TO MICROWAVE: Omit oil and decrease broth to ¾ cup. Toss pork, wine, soy sauce, 1 teaspoon cornstarch, the sugar and gingerroot in 2-quart microwavable casserole. Cover tightly and refrigerate 20 minutes. Microwave tightly covered on high 4 minutes; stir. Cover tightly and microwave until no longer pink, 3 to 4 minutes longer.

Stir in bell pepper, water chestnuts and broth. Mix cold water and 2 tablespoons cornstarch; stir into pork mixture. Cover tightly and microwave 2 minutes; stir. Cover tightly and microwave to boiling, 4 to 5 minutes, stirring every minute; stir in nectarines. Sprinkle with nuts. Serve with noodles. **4 servings**

PER SERVING: Calories 775; Protein 36 g; Carbohydrate 48 g; Fat 49 g; Cholesterol 90 mg; Sodium 670 mg

Gingered Pork with Nectarines

Stir-fried Pork with Pineapple

1 pound pork tenderloin
2 cans (8 ounces each) pineapple chunks
  in juice, drained and juice reserved
3 tablespoons white vinegar
3 tablespoons mirin (rice wine), sweet
  white wine or water
3 tablespoons reduced-sodium soy sauce
2 teaspoons cornstarch
1 teaspoon sesame oil
¼ cup coarsely chopped onion (about 1
  small)
1 medium green bell pepper, cut into
  1-inch pieces

Trim fat from pork tenderloin. Cut pork into 1-inch cubes. Mix reserved pineapple juice, the vinegar, mirin, soy sauce and cornstarch.

Spray wok or 12-inch nonstick skillet with nonstick cooking spray. Heat wok until hot. Add oil and pork; stir-fry 6 to 8 minutes or until pork is no longer pink. Remove pork from wok. Add onion and bell pepper to wok; stir-fry about 5 minutes or until onion is tender.

Stir pork, pineapple and cornstarch mixture into onion mixture. Heat to boiling. Boil about 45 seconds, stirring constantly, or until thickened. Serve over hot cooked rice or Chinese noodles if desired.   **4 servings**

PER SERVING: Calories 300; Protein 34 g; Carbohydrate 25 g; Fat 7 g; Cholesterol 105 mg; Sodium 530 mg

Sichuan Pork

1 pound pork boneless loin or leg
1 tablespoon soy sauce
2 teaspoons cornstarch
½ teaspoon ground red pepper (cayenne)
1 clove garlic, finely chopped
2 tablespoons vegetable oil
3 cups broccoli flowerets or 1 package
  (16 ounces) frozen chopped broccoli,
  thawed
2 small onions, cut into eighths
1 can (8 ounces) whole water chestnuts,
  drained
¼ cup chicken broth
½ cup peanuts
Hot cooked rice

Cut pork into slices, 2 × 1 × ⅛ inch. Toss pork, soy sauce, cornstarch, red pepper and garlic in glass or plastic bowl. Cover and refrigerate 20 minutes.

Heat 12-inch skillet or wok until 1 or 2 drops of water bubble and skitter when sprinkled in skillet. Add oil; rotate skillet to coat bottom. Add pork; cook and stir until no longer pink. Add broccoli, onions and water chestnuts; cook and stir 2 minutes. Stir in broth; heat to boiling. Stir in peanuts. Serve with rice.

PER SERVING: Calories 775; Protein 40 g; Carbohydrate 52 g; Fat 45 g; Cholesterol 90 mg; Sodium 870 mg

Sesame Pork

Texture is almost as important as flavor in this dish. Frying the meat twice gives it an exceptionally crisp exterior and a rich, deep color. The puffed, crunchy rice noodles are a perfect complement.

1¼ pounds pork boneless loin
1 egg, slightly beaten
2 tablespoons cornstarch
2 tablespoons vegetable oil
1 teaspoon salt
1 teaspoon light soy sauce
¼ teaspoon white pepper
2 tablespoons cornstarch
2 tablespoons water
2 tablespoons vegetable oil
2 teaspoons dried ground chile
2 teaspoons finely chopped garlic
1 teaspoon finely chopped gingerroot
¾ cup sugar
¾ cup chicken broth
⅔ cup vinegar
2 teaspoons dark soy sauce
Vegetable oil
2 ounces rice stick noodles
¾ cup all-purpose flour
¾ cup water
3 tablespoons cornstarch
1 tablespoon salt
1 teaspoon baking soda
3 tablespoons toasted sesame seed
2 tablespoons chopped green onion (with tops)

Trim fat from pork loin; cut pork into ¾-inch pieces. Mix egg, 2 tablespoons cornstarch, 2 tablespoons oil, 1 teaspoon salt, 1 teaspoon light soy sauce and the white pepper in medium glass or plastic bowl; stir in pork. Cover and refrigerate 30 minutes.

Mix 2 tablespoons cornstarch and 2 tablespoons water. Heat 2 tablespoons oil over medium heat in 2-quart saucepan; reduce heat to low. Add chile, garlic, and gingerroot; cook 30 seconds. Add sugar, broth, vinegar and 2 teaspoons dark soy sauce; heat to boiling. Add cornstarch mixture; cook and stir 15 seconds or until thickened. Keep sauce warm.

Heat oil (1 inch) in wok to 425°. Fry noodles, ¼ at a time, 5 seconds or until puffed, turning once; drain on paper towels.

Reduce oil temperature to 350°. Mix flour, ¾ cup water, 3 tablespoons cornstarch, 1 tablespoon salt and the baking soda. Stir pork into batter until pork is well coated. Fry 15 to 18 pieces of pork at a time 4 minutes or until light brown, turning occasionally; drain on paper towels.

Increase oil temperature to 375°. Fry pork all at one time 1 minute or until golden brown; drain on paper towels. Place noodles on heated platter. Mix pork with sauce; pour over noodles. Sprinkle with sesame seed and onions.

4 to 6 servings

PER SERVING: Calories 985; Protein 46 g; Carbohydrate 81 g; Fat 53 g; Cholesterol 180 mg; Sodium 2870 mg

Oriental Pork and Cabbage

To toast sesame seed, heat in ungreased skillet over medium heat about 2 minutes, stirring occasionally, until golden brown.

1 pound lean pork tenderloin
2 teaspoons low-sodium soy sauce
1 teaspoon sesame oil
1 teaspoon cornstarch
1 teaspoon sugar
⅛ teaspoon pepper
2 cloves garlic, finely chopped
3 teaspoons vegetable oil
2 cups coarsely shredded cabbage (about 8 ounces)
1 medium bell pepper, cut into ¼-inch strips
1 cup 1-inch pieces green onions (with tops)
1 tablespoon sesame seed, toasted

Trim fat from pork tenderloin. Cut pork with grain into 2-inch strips. Cut strips across grain into ¼-inch slices. (For ease in cutting, partially freeze pork, about 1½ hours.) Toss pork, soy sauce, sesame oil, cornstarch, sugar, pepper and garlic in medium glass or plastic bowl or heavy plastic bag. Cover and refrigerate 30 minutes.

Heat 1 teaspoon of the oil in 10-inch nonstick skillet over medium-high heat until hot. Add pork; stir-fry 4 to 5 minutes or until pork is brown. Remove pork from the skillet.

Heat remaining 2 teaspoons oil in skillet until hot. Add cabbage, bell pepper and onions; stir-fry 2 minutes. Stir in pork; heat until hot. Top with sesame seed.   **4 servings**

PER SERVING: Calories 235; Protein 27 g; Carbohydrate 9 g; Fat 10 g; Cholesterol 80 mg; Sodium 180 mg

Sichuan Stir-fried Pork with Vegetables

2 teaspoons cornstarch
2 teaspoons cold water
1 pound pork for stir-fry or chow mein
1 teaspoon cornstarch
1 teaspoon soy sauce
½ teaspoon salt
⅛ teaspoon white pepper
2 tablespoons vegetable oil
1 clove garlic, finely chopped
3 cups cut-up vegetables for stir-fry
2 teaspoons chile paste or chile puree with garlic*
¼ cup chicken broth or water

Mix 2 teaspoons cornstarch and the water; reserve. Toss pork, 1 teaspoon cornstarch, the soy sauce, salt and white pepper.

Heat wok or 12-inch skillet until 1 or 2 drops of water bubble and skitter when sprinkled in wok. Add oil; rotate wok to coat sides. Add pork and garlic; stir-fry until pork is no longer pink. Add vegetables; stir-fry 2 minutes. Stir in chile paste. Stir in broth; heat to boiling. Stir in reserved cornstarch mixture. Cook and stir about 10 seconds or until thickened.

*1 teaspoon finely chopped dried chile pepper and 1 tablespoon soy sauce can be substituted for the chile paste.

PER SERVING: Calories 385; Protein 23 g; Carbohydrate 10 g; Fat 28 g; Cholesterol 70 mg; Sodium 500 mg

Stir-fried Pork and Pasta

If you like, substitute other thin pasta, such as spaghetti or angel hair pasta, for the vermicelli.

1¼ pounds pork boneless loin or leg
1 teaspoon cornstarch
1 teaspoon soy sauce
¼ teaspoon salt
⅛ teaspoon pepper
2 tablespoons vegetable oil
2 large cloves garlic, finely chopped
¼ to ½ teaspoon finely crushed dried red pepper
2 medium stalks celery, diagonally cut into ¼-inch slices (about 1 cup)
1 small green bell pepper, cut into 1-inch pieces
2 cups bean sprouts (about 4 ounces)
4 ounces mushrooms, sliced (about 1¼ cups)
2 cups cooked vermicelli (about 4 ounces uncooked)
3 green onions (with tops), sliced
1 tablespoon soy sauce

Trim fat from pork. Cut pork into strips, 2 × 1 × ⅛ inch. (For ease in cutting, partially freeze pork, about 1½ hours.) Toss pork, cornstarch, 1 teaspoon soy sauce, the salt and pepper in glass or plastic bowl. Cover and refrigerate 20 minutes.

Heat oil in 12-inch skillet or wok over high heat until hot. Add pork, garlic and red pepper; cook and stir until pork is no longer pink, about 5 minutes. Add celery and bell pepper; cook and stir 2 minutes. Add bean sprouts and mushrooms; cook and stir 2 minutes. Add vermicelli, green onions and 1 tablespoon soy sauce; toss until thoroughly mixed, about 2 minutes.

6 servings

PER SERVING: Calories 375; Protein 31 g; Carbohydrate 18 g; Fat 20 g; Cholesterol 85 mg; Sodium 460 mg

Stir-fried Noodles with Sichuan Sauce

If you prefer a less spicy dish, reduce or omit the red pepper sauce.

6 medium dried black mushrooms
2 tablespoons cornstarch
2 tablespoons water
2 teaspoons red pepper sauce
2 quarts water
6 ounces Chinese egg noodles or linguini
2 tablespoons vegetable oil
2 tablespoons vegetable oil
10 ounces lean ground pork
2 tablespoons brown bean sauce
1 tablespoon finely chopped garlic
2 cups chicken broth
2 teaspoons dark soy sauce
1 teaspoon sesame oil
2 tablespoons diced pimiento
1 tablespoon chopped green onion

Soak mushrooms in hot water 20 minutes or until soft; drain. Rinse in warm water; drain. Squeeze out excess moisture. Remove and discard stems; cut caps into ¼-inch pieces. Mix cornstarch, 2 tablespoons water and the pepper sauce.

Heat 2 quarts water to boiling in Dutch oven; stir in noodles. Heat to boiling; reduce heat to medium. Cook uncovered 5 minutes or until done; drain. Rinse in cold water; drain well. (If using linguini, cook as directed on package.)

Heat wok until very hot. Add 2 tablespoons oil; tilt wok to coat side. Reduce heat to medium. Add noodles; cook until light brown, using a fork to separate and flip noodles as they cook. (If noodles are not browning and appear to be dry, add 1 tablespoon oil.) Remove noodles to heat-proof platter; keep warm in 300° oven.

Heat wok until very hot. Add 2 tablespoons oil; tilt wok to coat side. Add pork; stir-fry until pork is no longer pink. Add mushrooms, bean sauce and garlic; stir-fry 1 minute. Add broth; heat to boiling. Stir in cornstarch mixture; cook and stir until thickened. Stir in soy sauce, sesame oil and pimiento; cook and stir 15 seconds. Pour pork mixture over noodles; sprinkle with green onion. **4 servings**

PER SERVING: Calories 460; Protein 17 g; Carbohydrate 30 g; Fat 29 g; Cholesterol 45 mg; Sodium 660 mg

Stir-fried Noodles with Sichuan Sauce

Sweet-and-Sour Pork

1½ pounds pork boneless loin or leg
1 egg, slightly beaten
2 tablespoons cornstarch
2 tablespoons vegetable oil
1 teaspoon salt
1 teaspoon light soy sauce
¼ teaspoon white pepper
2 tomatoes
1 green bell pepper
Vegetable oil
¾ cup all-purpose flour
¾ cup water
2 tablespoons cornstarch
1 teaspoon salt
1 teaspoon baking soda
1 cup plus 2 tablespoons sugar
1 cup chicken broth
¾ cup white vinegar
1 tablespoon vegetable oil
2 teaspoons dark soy sauce
1 teaspoon salt
1 clove garlic, finely chopped
¼ cup cornstarch
¼ cup cold water
1 can (8¼ ounces) pineapple chunks,
   drained

Trim fat from pork; cut pork into ¾-inch pieces. Mix egg, 2 tablespoons cornstarch, 2 tablespoons oil, 1 teaspoon salt, 1 teaspoon light soy sauce and the white pepper in medium glass or plastic bowl; stir in pork. Cover and refrigerate 20 minutes.

Cut each tomato into 8 wedges. Cut bell pepper into 1-inch pieces.

Heat oil (1½ inches) in wok to 350°. Mix flour, ¾ cup water, 2 tablespoons cornstarch, 1 teaspoon salt and the baking soda in medium bowl. Stir pork pieces into batter until well coated. Fry about 15 pieces at a time 4 minutes or until light brown, turning frequently; drain on paper towels. Increase oil temperature to 375°. Fry pork all at one time 1 minute or until golden brown; drain on paper towels. Place pork on heated platter.

Heat sugar, broth, vinegar, 1 tablespoon oil, 2 teaspoons dark soy sauce, 1 teaspoon salt and the garlic to boiling in 3-quart saucepan. Mix ¼ cup cornstarch and ¼ cup water; stir into sauce. Cook and stir about 20 seconds or until thickened. Stir in tomatoes, bell pepper and pineapple. Heat to boiling; pour over pork.

8 servings

PER SERVING: Calories 535; Protein 26 g; Carbohydrate 52 g; Fat 25 g; Cholesterol 105 mg; Sodium 1200 mg

Sweet-and-Sour Pork

Shredded Pork with Bean Sprouts

1 pound pork boneless loin or leg
1 tablespoon cornstarch
½ teaspoon salt
⅛ teaspoon white pepper
6 medium dried black mushrooms
1 pound bean sprouts
4 green onions (with tops)
1 tablespoon cornstarch
1 teaspoon sugar
2 teaspoons light soy sauce
2 tablespoons vegetable oil
1 teaspoon finely chopped garlic
½ teaspoon salt
¼ cup chicken broth

Trim fat from pork loin; cut pork with grain into 2 × 1-inch strips. Cut strips across grain into ⅛-inch slices. Stack slices; cut into thin strips. (For ease in cutting, partially freeze pork, about 1½ hours.) Toss pork, 1 tablespoon cornstarch, ½ teaspoon salt and the white pepper in medium bowl. Cover and refrigerate 30 minutes.

Soak mushrooms in hot water 20 minutes or until soft; drain. Rinse in warm water; drain. Squeeze out excess moisture. Remove and discard stems; cut caps into ½-inch strips.

Rinse bean sprouts in cold water; drain. Cut onions diagonally into 1-inch pieces. Mix 1 tablespoon cornstarch, the sugar and soy sauce.

Heat wok until very hot. Add oil; tilt wok to coat side. Add pork; stir-fry 2 minutes or until pork is no longer pink. Add mushrooms, garlic, and ½ teaspoon salt; stir-fry 30 seconds. Add bean sprouts and green onions; stir-fry 2 minutes. Stir in broth; heat to boiling. Stir in cornstarch mixture; cook and stir 15 seconds or until thickened. **4 servings**

PER SERVING: Calories 535; Protein 46 g; Carbohydrate 20 g; Fat 30 g; Cholesterol 100 mg; Sodium 850 mg

Marinated-Pork Fried Rice

½ pound pork tenderloin
¼ cup unsweetened pineapple juice
½ teaspoon grated gingerroot or ¼ teaspoon ground ginger
¼ teaspoon red pepper sauce
1 clove garlic, crushed
½ cup chopped onion (about 1 medium)
½ cup chopped red bell pepper (about 1 small)
2 tablespoons reduced-sodium soy sauce or fish sauce
3 cups cold cooked rice

Trim fat from pork tenderloin. Cut pork into ½-inch cubes. Mix pork, pineapple juice, gingerroot, pepper sauce and garlic in glass or plastic bowl. Cover and refrigerate at least 1 hour but no longer than 12 hours.

Spray wok or 12-inch nonstick skillet with nonstick cooking spray. Heat wok until hot. Remove pork from marinade; drain. Add pork to wok; stir-fry 5 to 10 minutes or until no longer pink. Remove pork from wok.

Add onion and bell pepper to wok; stir-fry about 8 minutes or until onion is tender. Stir in pork and remaining ingredients. Cook about 10 minutes, stirring constantly, until rice is hot and golden. Sprinkle with chopped fresh chives and serve with additional soy sauce if desired.

4 servings

PER SERVING: Calories 305; Protein 21 g; Carbohydrate 48 g; Fat 3 g; Cholesterol 55 mg; Sodium 340 mg

Pork and Tofu Stir-fry

Tofu, the curd made from soybeans, has the most protein for its calories of all legume products. Without an assertive flavor of its own, it is a nice carrier for seasonings and sauces.

½ **pound lean pork boneless loin or leg**
1 **teaspoon cornstarch**
1 **teaspoon low-sodium soy sauce**
1 **cup Chinese pea pods (about 3½ ounces)**
2 **teaspoons vegetable oil**
1 **teaspoon finely chopped gingerroot or ½ teaspoon ground ginger**
1 **clove garlic, finely chopped**
1 **cup sliced fresh mushrooms (about 3 ounces)**
¼ **cup sliced green onions (with tops)**
2 **teaspoons oyster sauce**
1 **teaspoon low-sodium soy sauce**
5 **ounces firm tofu, cut into ½-inch cubes**

Trim fat from pork loin. Cut pork into 2 × 1 × ⅛-inch slices. (For ease in cutting, partially freeze pork, about 1½ hours.) Toss pork, cornstarch and 1 teaspoon soy sauce in medium glass or plastic bowl. Cover and refrigerate 20 minutes. Heat 1 inch water to boiling in 1½-quart saucepan. Add pea pods. Cover and boil 1 minute; drain. Immediately rinse with cold water; drain.

Heat oil in 10-inch nonstick skillet or wok over high heat. Add pork mixture, gingerroot and garlic; stir-fry about 3 minutes or until pork is no longer pink. Add mushrooms and onions; stir-fry 2 minutes longer. Add remaining ingredients; stir-fry until heated through and mixed thoroughly. **4 servings**

PER SERVING: Calories 165; Protein 15 g; Carbohydrate 7 g; Fat 9 g; Cholesterol 35 mg; Sodium 130 mg

Italian Sausage and Vegetables

Try cutting the spaghetti squash crosswise; you'll have longer strands than if you cut it lengthwise.

1 **spaghetti squash (about 3 pounds)**
1 **pound Italian sausage, casing removed and sausage crumbled, or bulk Italian sausage**
½ **cup chopped onion (about 1 medium)**
1 **cup coarsely chopped zucchini (about 1 medium)**
¼ **cup chopped fresh parsley**
1 **large clove garlic, crushed**
3 **tablespoons chopped fresh or 1 tablespoon dried basil leaves**
3 **cups coarsely chopped tomatoes (about 3 large)**
⅓ **cup grated Parmesan cheese**
½ **teaspoon salt**
¼ **teaspoon pepper**

Heat oven to 400°. Prick squash with fork. Bake about 1 hour or until tender.

Cook sausage and onion in 10-inch nonstick skillet over medium heat about 10 minutes, stirring occasionally, until sausage is done; drain. Stir in zucchini, parsley, garlic and basil. Cover and cook 3 minutes. Stir in tomatoes and cheese. Cut squash into halves; remove seeds and fibers. Remove spaghetti-like strands, using 2 forks; toss with salt and pepper. Serve sausage mixture over squash. **6 servings**

PER SERVING: Calories 275; Protein 17 g; Carbohydrate 18 g; Fat 16 g; Cholesterol 18 mg; Sodium 790 mg

Stir-fried Spareribs with Green Peppers

Stir-fried Spareribs with Green Peppers

Spareribs make a fun stir-fry, and the do-ahead directions let you make dinner ahead of time, then cook it quickly when you're ready.

2- to 3-pound rack pork ribs, cut length-wise across bones into halves
2 teaspoons cornstarch
2 teaspoons soy sauce
1 teaspoon salt
1 teaspoon sugar
2 green bell peppers
2 green onions (with tops)
2 tablespoons vegetable oil
2 cloves garlic, finely chopped
1 teaspoon finely chopped gingerroot
2 tablespoons brown bean sauce
1 cup chicken broth
¼ cup cold water
2 tablespoons cornstarch
1 teaspoon sugar

Trim fat and remove membranes from ribs; cut between each rib to separate. Toss ribs, 2 teaspoons cornstarch, the soy sauce, salt and 1 teaspoon sugar in glass or plastic bowl. Cover and refrigerate 30 minutes. Cut bell peppers into 1-inch pieces. Cut green onions into 2-inch pieces.

Heat wok until 1 or 2 drops of water bubble and skitter when sprinkled in wok. Add vegetable oil; rotate wok to coat side. Add ribs, garlic and gingerroot; stir-fry 2 minutes. Add bean sauce; stir-fry 1 minute. Stir in broth. Heat to boiling; reduce heat. Cover and simmer 20 minutes.

Mix water, 2 tablespoons cornstarch and 1 teaspoon sugar; stir into ribs. Cook and stir until thickened. Add green peppers; cook and stir 1 minute. Garnish with green onions.

4 servings

DO-AHEAD DIRECTIONS: After simmering ribs 20 minutes, cover and refrigerate no longer than 24 hours. Just before serving, heat ribs to boiling; cover and cook 2 minutes. Continue as directed.

PER SERVING: Calories 585; Protein 27 g; Carbohydrate 16 g; Fat 46 g; Cholesterol 105 mg; Sodium 1360 mg

Sweet-and-Sour Ham

1 medium onion, sliced
2 teaspoons margarine or butter
1 can (15¼ ounces) pineapple chunks in juice, drained and juice reserved
2½ cups cut-up fully cooked smoked reduced-sodium ham (about ¾ pound)
½ cup chopped bell pepper (about 1 small)
¼ teaspoon pepper
1 tablespoon cornstarch
2 tablespoons cold water
2 cups hot cooked brown rice

Cook onion in margarine in 10-inch nonstick skillet over medium heat about 5 minutes, stirring frequently, until onion is tender. Add enough water to reserved pineapple juice to measure 1 cup. Stir pineapple juice, pineapple, ham, bell pepper and pepper into onion. Heat to boiling; reduce heat. Cover and simmer about 5 minutes or until bell pepper is crisp-tender. Mix cornstarch and cold water; gradually stir into ham mixture. Heat to boiling, stirring constantly. Boil and stir 1 minute. Serve over rice.

4 servings

PER SERVING: Calories 365; Protein 23 g; Carbohydrate 44 g; Fat 11 g; Cholesterol 50 mg; Sodium 934 mg

Spicy Chicken with Broccoli

2

Chicken

Spicy Chicken with Broccoli

If you like, you can substitute 4 boneless skinless chicken breasts (about 1 pound) for the whole chicken breasts.

2 whole chicken breasts (about 2 pounds)
2 teaspoons cornstarch
½ teaspoon salt
¼ teaspoon white pepper
1 pound broccoli
3 green onions (with tops)
1 hot green chile or 1 teaspoon dried red pepper flakes
3 tablespoons vegetable oil
2 tablespoons brown bean sauce
2 teaspoons finely chopped garlic
1 teaspoon sugar
1 teaspoon finely chopped gingerroot

Remove bones and skin from chicken breasts; cut chicken into 2 × ½-inch pieces. Toss chicken, cornstarch, salt and white pepper in medium bowl. Cover and refrigerate 20 minutes.

Pare outer layer from broccoli. Cut broccoli lengthwise into 1-inch-thick stems; remove flowerets. Cut stems diagonally into ¼-inch slices. Place broccoli flowerets and stems in boiling water; heat to boiling. Cover and cook 1 minute; drain. Immediately rinse in cold water; drain. Cut green onions diagonally into 1-inch pieces. Remove seeds and membranes from chile. Cut chile into very thin slices.

Heat wok until very hot. Add oil; tilt wok to coat side. Add chile, brown bean sauce, garlic, sugar and gingerroot; stir-fry 10 seconds. Add chicken; stir-fry 2 minutes or until chicken is white. Add broccoli and green onions; stir-fry 1 minute or until broccoli is hot. **4 servings**

PER SERVING: Calories 335; Protein 39 g; Carbohydrate 11 g; Fat 15 g; Cholesterol 90 mg; Sodium 440 mg

Chicken with Celery

To cut the hot green chile, hold the stem and cut off the tip with scissors. Loosen the membranes and seeds with tip of scissor blade; discard. Cut chile into slices with scissors.

2 whole chicken breasts (about 2 pounds)
2 teaspoons cornstarch
½ teaspoon salt
¼ teaspoon white pepper
5 stalks celery
3 green onions (with tops)
1 hot green chile or 1 teaspoon dried red pepper flakes
3 tablespoons vegetable oil
2 tablespoons brown bean sauce
2 teaspoons finely chopped garlic
1 teaspoon finely chopped gingerroot

Remove bones and skin from chicken breasts; cut chicken into 2 × ½-inch strips. Toss chicken, cornstarch, salt and white pepper in medium bowl. Cover and refrigerate 20 minutes.

Cut celery diagonally into ¼-inch slices. Place celery in boiling water; heat to boiling. Boil 1 minute; drain. Immediately rinse in cold water; drain. Cut onions diagonally into 1-inch pieces. Remove stems and membranes from chile. Cut chile into very thin slices.

Heat wok until very hot. Add oil; tilt wok to coat side. Add bean sauce, chile, garlic and gingerroot; stir-fry 10 seconds. Add chicken; stir-fry until chicken turns white. Add green onions and celery; stir-fry 1 minute.   **4 servings**

PER SERVING: Calories 305; Protein 36 g; Carbohydrate 6 g; Fat 15 g; Cholesterol 90 mg; Sodium 460 mg

Stir-fried Chicken

2 whole chicken breasts (about 2 pounds)
1 egg white
1 teaspoon cornstarch
1 teaspoon soy sauce
½ teaspoon salt
3 medium zucchinis
2 tablespoons cornstarch
2 tablespoons cold water
3 tablespoons vegetable oil
1 medium onion, thinly sliced
2 large cloves garlic, finely chopped
1 teaspoon finely chopped gingerroot
8 ounces mushrooms, sliced (about 3 cups)
½ cup chicken broth
2 tablespoons soy sauce

Remove skin and bones from chicken; cut chicken into strips, 2 × 1 inch. Mix egg white, 1 teaspoon cornstarch, 1 teaspoon soy sauce and the salt in 1½-quart glass or plastic bowl; stir in chicken. Cover and refrigerate 20 minutes.

Cut zucchinis lengthwise into halves; cut each half diagonally into ¼-inch slices. Mix 2 tablespoons cornstarch and the water; reserve.

Heat oil in 12-inch skillet or wok over high heat until hot. Add chicken; cook and stir until chicken turns white, about 3 minutes. Remove chicken from skillet. Add onion, garlic and gingerroot; cook and stir until garlic is brown. Add zucchini and mushrooms; cook and stir 2 minutes. Stir in chicken, broth and 2 tablespoons soy sauce; heat to boiling. Stir in cornstarch mixture. Boil and stir 1 minute.   **6 servings**

PER SERVING: Calories 250; Protein 27 g; Carbohydrate 13 g; Fat 10 g; Cholesterol 60 mg; Sodium 710 mg

Stir-fried Chicken with Bean Sprouts

Bean sprouts add a lovely crunch—and they need no chopping—to this delectable stir-fry.

6 medium dried black mushrooms
2 whole chicken breasts (about 2 pounds)
1 egg white
1 teaspoon cornstarch
1 teaspoon salt
1 teaspoon light soy sauce
Dash of white pepper
1 pound bean sprouts
6 green onions (with tops)
¼ cup sugar
¼ cup oyster sauce
2 tablespoons cornstarch
2 tablespoons cold water
¼ cup vegetable oil
1 teaspoon finely chopped garlic
1 teaspoon grated gingerroot
2 tablespoons vegetable oil
½ cup chicken broth

Soak mushrooms in warm water until soft, about 30 minutes; drain. Rinse in warm water; drain. Remove and discard stems; cut caps into thin slices. Remove skin and bones from chicken; cut chicken into strips, 2 × 1 inch. Mix egg white, 1 teaspoon cornstarch, the salt, soy sauce and white pepper in glass or plastic bowl; stir in chicken. Cover and refrigerate 20 minutes.

Rinse bean sprouts in cold water; drain. Cut green onions into 2-inch pieces; cut lengthwise into thin strips. Mix sugar, oyster sauce, 2 tablespoons cornstarch and the water.

Heat wok until 1 or 2 drops of water bubble and skitter when sprinkled in wok. Add ¼ cup vegetable oil; rotate wok to coat side. Add chicken, garlic and gingerroot; stir-fry until chicken turns white. Remove chicken from wok.

Add 2 tablespoons oil to wok; rotate to coat side. Add mushrooms and bean sprouts; stir-fry 1 minute. Stir in chicken and broth; heat to boiling. Stir in cornstarch mixture; cook and stir until thickened, about 30 seconds. Stir in green onions. **6 servings**

PER SERVING: Calories 440; Protein 36 g; Carbohydrate 24 g; Fat 22 g; Cholesterol 60 mg; Sodium 1010 mg

Chicken and Peppers

2 medium green bell peppers, cut into ¼-inch strips
1 small onion, chopped (about ¼ cup)
1 clove garlic, finely chopped
2 tablespoons vegetable oil
4 small chicken breast halves (about 2 pounds), skinned, boned, and cut into 1-inch pieces, or 1 pound turkey tenderloin, cut into 1-inch pieces
1 teaspoon salt
⅛ teaspoon pepper
Lemon wedges

Cook and stir bell peppers, onion and garlic in oil in 10-inch skillet over medium-high heat until peppers are almost tender, about 5 minutes. Add chicken, salt and pepper. Cook and stir until chicken is done, about 8 minutes. Serve with lemon wedges. **4 servings**

CHICKEN CILANTRO: Omit bell peppers. Stir 2 tablespoons snipped cilantro into the cooked chicken.

PER SERVING: Calories 260; Protein 36 g; Carbohydrate 4 g; Fat 11 g; Cholesterol 90 mg; Sodium 620 mg

Stir-fried Chicken and Vegetables

To make slicing raw chicken easier, partially freeze it for about 1½ hours.

4 skinless boneless chicken breast
    halves (about 1 pound), cut into 1½ ×
    ¼-inch strips
1 egg white
1 teaspoon cornstarch
1 teaspoon reduced-sodium soy sauce
6 ounces chinese pea pods or 1 package
    (6 ounces) frozen Chinese pea pods,
    partially thawed
1 tablespoon vegetable oil
2 cloves garlic, finely chopped
1 teaspoon finely chopped gingerroot
3 cups ¼-inch diagonal slices celery
    (about 6 medium stalks)
2 cups sliced mushrooms (about 6
    ounces)
1 can (8 ounces) sliced water chestnuts,
    drained
1 can (8 ounces) sliced bamboo shoots,
    drained
1 tablespoon vegetable oil
¾ cup chicken broth
½ teaspoon sugar
¼ cup cold water
2 tablespoons cornstarch
1 teaspoon reduced-sodium soy sauce

Mix chicken, egg white, 1 teaspoon cornstarch and 1 teaspoon soy sauce in glass or plastic bowl. Cover and refrigerate 30 minutes.

Meanwhile, remove strings from fresh pea pods or rinse frozen pea pods with cold water to separate; drain. Heat 1 tablespoon oil in wok or 12-inch nonstick skillet until hot. Add garlic and gingerroot; stir-fry over medium heat until light brown. Add pea pods and celery; stir-fry 1 minute. Add mushrooms, water chestnuts and bamboo shoots; stir-fry 1 minute. Remove vegetables with slotted spoon.

Heat 1 tablespoon oil in wok until hot. Add chicken; stir-fry over high heat about 2 minutes or until white. Stir in broth and sugar. Heat to boiling; reduce heat. Cover and simmer 2 minutes, stirring occasionally. Mix cold water, 2 tablespoons cornstarch and 1 teaspoon soy sauce; stir into chicken mixture. Heat to boiling, stirring constantly. Boil and stir 1 minute. Add vegetables; cook and stir 1 to 2 minutes or until hot. **4 servings**

PER SERVING: Calories 315; Protein 32 g; Carbohydrate 22 g; Fat 11 g; Cholesterol 65 mg; Sodium 390 mg

Stir-fried Chicken with Mushrooms

For help in deboning chicken breasts, see page 43.

2 whole chicken breasts (about 2
    pounds)
1 egg white
1 teaspoon cornstarch
1 teaspoon salt
1 teaspoon light soy sauce
Dash of white pepper
1 pound mushrooms
4 ounces pea pods
2 tablespoons cornstarch
2 tablespoons cold water
3 tablespoons vegetable oil
2 cloves garlic, finely chopped
1 teaspoon finely chopped gingerroot
2 tablespoons vegetable oil
½ cup chicken broth
1 tablespoon oyster sauce

Remove skin and bones from chicken; cut chicken into ¼-inch slices. Mix egg white, 1 teaspoon cornstarch, the salt, the soy sauce and white pepper in glass or plastic bowl; stir in chicken. Cover and refrigerate 30 minutes.

Cut mushrooms into ½-inch slices. Remove strings from pea pods. Place pea pods in boiling water. Cover and boil 1 minute; drain. Immediately rinse under running cold water; drain. Mix 2 tablespoons cornstarch and the water.

Heat wok until 1 or 2 drops of water bubble and skitter when sprinkled in wok. Add 3 tablespoons vegetable oil; rotate wok to coat side. Add chicken, garlic and gingerroot; stir-fry until chicken turns white. Remove chicken from wok.

Add 2 tablespoons oil to wok; rotate to coat side. Add mushrooms; stir-fry 1 minute. Stir in chicken and broth; heat to boiling. Stir in cornstarch mixture; cook and stir until thickened, about 10 seconds. Add pea pods and oyster sauce; cook and stir 30 seconds.   **6 servings.**

MICROWAVE REHEAT DIRECTIONS: Prepare Stir-fried Chicken with Mushrooms; cover and refrigerate no longer than 24 hours. Cover tightly and microwave on microwavable platter or bowl on high 4 minutes; stir. Cover and microwave until hot, 5 minutes longer.

PER SERVING: Calories 280; Protein 27 g; Carbohydrate 9 g; Fat 15 g; Cholesterol 60 mg; Sodium 670 mg

Boning a Chicken Breast

1. Remove skin from a whole chicken breast. Place meaty side down on a clean, dry cutting surface. Cut just through the white cartilage at the V of the neck to expose the end of the keel bone (the dark bone at the center of the breast).

2. Bend the breast halves back until the keel bone pops away from the meat. Run a finger along each side of the keel bone to loosen it. Pull the bone out; if it comes out in pieces, that is fine.

3. To remove the rib cages, insert the point of the knife under the long rib bone. Cut the rib cage away from the meat. Cut through the shoulder joint to free the entire rib cage.

4. To cut away the wishbone, slip the knife under the white tendons on either side of the breast; loosen and pull out the tendons. Cut the breast into halves.

Creamy Spinach and Chicken Dinner

The presentation of chicken on beds of spinach makes this an elegant dish. The nutmeg adds a lovely note to the overall flavor.

6 skinless boneless chicken breast halves (about 1½ pounds)
1 cup low-fat milk
½ cup chicken broth
½ cup chopped onion (about 1 medium)
7 cups chopped spinach (about 9 ounces)
¼ teaspoon salt
¼ teaspoon pepper
¼ teaspoon ground nutmeg

Spray 12-inch skillet with nonstick cooking spray. Heat skillet over medium heat. Cook chicken in skillet 2 minutes on each side. Reduce heat to medium-low. Add milk, broth and onion. Cook 5 minutes, turning chicken occasionally, until onion is tender. Add spinach. Cook 3 to 4 minutes, stirring occasionally, until spinach is completely wilted and juices of chicken run clear. Remove chicken from skillet; keep warm. Increase heat to medium. Cook spinach mixture about 3 minutes or until liquid has almost evaporated. Stir in salt, pepper and nutmeg. Serve chicken on top of spinach.

6 servings

PER SERVING: Calories 170; Protein 28 g; Carbohydrate 6 g; Fat 4 g; Cholesterol 65 mg; Sodium 280 mg

Orange Stir-fried Chicken

4 boneless skinless chicken breast halves (about 1 pound)
1 tablespoon low-sodium or regular soy sauce
1 teaspoon cornstarch
1 teaspoon grated gingerroot or ½ teaspoon ground ginger
1 clove garlic, finely chopped
½ cup orange juice
2 teaspoons cornstarch
2 teaspoons vegetable oil
3 cups thinly sliced fresh mushrooms (about 8 ounces)
½ cup coarsely shredded carrot (about 1 medium)
2 cups hot cooked rice

Trim fat from chicken breast halves. Cut chicken into ¼-inch strips. Mix soy sauce, 1 teaspoon cornstarch, the gingerroot and garlic in medium glass or plastic bowl. Stir in chicken. Cover and refrigerate 30 minutes.

Mix orange juice and 2 teaspoons cornstarch until cornstarch is dissolved. Heat 1 teaspoon of the oil in 10-inch nonstick skillet over high heat. Add chicken mixture; stir-fry until chicken turns white. Remove chicken from skillet.

Add remaining 1 teaspoon oil to skillet. Add mushrooms and carrot; stir-fry about 3 minutes or until mushrooms are tender. Stir in chicken and orange juice mixture. Heat to boiling, stirring constantly. Boil and stir 30 seconds or until thickened. Serve over rice.   **4 servings**

PER SERVING: Calories 315; Protein 28 g; Carbohydrate 35 g; Fat 6 g; Cholesterol 80 mg; Sodium 630 mg

Orange Stir-fried Chicken

Lemon Chicken

There are a number of different Lemon Chicken recipes. This popular version develops an intense lemony flavor without lengthy marinating. After frying, you can refrigerate the chicken for 24 hours if you like. Make the sauce ahead, too, if it's more convenient. Just before serving, heat oil to 375° and fry chicken, turning once or twice, for about 2 minutes. Reheat sauce to boiling and serve over chicken.

2 whole chicken breasts (about 2 pounds)
1 egg
2 teaspoons cornstarch
1 teaspoon salt
¼ teaspoon white pepper
1 teaspoon finely chopped gingerroot
1 tablespoon cornstarch
1 tablespoon water
Vegetable oil
¼ cup all-purpose flour
¼ cup water
2 tablespoons cornstarch
2 tablespoons vegetable oil
¼ teaspoon baking soda
¼ teaspoon salt
½ cup chicken broth
¼ cup sugar
3 tablespoons lemon juice
2 tablespoons light corn syrup
2 tablespoons vinegar
1 tablespoon vegetable oil
1 teaspoon dark soy sauce
1 teaspoon finely chopped garlic
½ lemon, thinly sliced

Remove skin and bones from chicken breasts; cut each chicken breast lengthwise into fourths. Place chicken in a shallow dish. Mix egg, 2 teaspoons cornstarch, 1 teaspoon salt, the white pepper and gingerroot. Pour egg mixture over chicken, turning chicken to coat all sides. Cover and refrigerate 30 minutes. Remove chicken from marinade; reserve marinade. Mix 1 tablespoon cornstarch and 1 tablespoon water.

Heat oil (1½ inches) in wok to 350°. Mix reserved marinade, the flour, ¼ cup water, 2 tablespoons cornstarch, 2 tablespoons vegetable oil, the baking soda and ¼ teaspoon salt. Dip chicken pieces, one at a time, into batter to coat all sides. Fry 2 pieces at a time 3 minutes or until light brown; drain on paper towels.

Increase oil temperature to 375°. Fry all the chicken 2 minutes or until golden brown, turning once; drain on paper towels. Cut each piece crosswise into ½-inch pieces, using a very sharp knife; place in a single layer on heated platter.

Heat broth, sugar, lemon juice, corn syrup, vinegar, 1 tablespoon oil, the soy sauce and garlic to boiling. Stir in cornstarch mixture; cook and stir 10 seconds or until thickened. Simmer uncovered 30 seconds. Pour sauce over chicken; garnish with lemon slices and, if desired, maraschino cherries or cilantro. **6 servings**

PER SERVING: Calories 365; Protein 25 g; Carbohydrate 24 g; Fat 19 g; Cholesterol 60 mg; Sodium 650 mg

Orange-glazed Chicken and Carrots

Wild rice adds a touch of elegance to this easy dinner.

1 package (6¾ ounces) instant long
  grain and wild rice
1 tablespoon vegetable oil
2 large boneless skinless chicken breast
  halves (about ¾ pound), cut into 1½-
  inch pieces
1 package (16 ounces) frozen whole baby
  carrots
1 can (6 ounces) frozen orange juice con-
  centrate, thawed
1 juice can water
2 tablespoons honey
2 tablespoons cornstarch
1 teaspoon dry mustard
2 tablespoons cold water

Prepare instant rice as directed on package; keep warm. Heat oil in 10-inch skillet over medium heat until hot. Cook and stir chicken in oil until white.

Stir in carrots, orange juice, juice can water and honey. Heat to boiling; reduce heat to medium. Cook uncovered, stirring occasionally, until carrots are done, 10 to 12 minutes.

Mix cornstarch and mustard; stir in cold water. Stir into chicken mixture. Heat to boiling, stirring constantly. Boil and stir 1 minute. Serve with rice. **4 servings**

PER SERVING: Calories 435; Protein 39 g; Carbohydrate 52 g; Fat 8 g; Cholesterol 90 mg; Sodium 320 mg

Sweet-and-Sour Chicken

½ cup pineapple juice
2 tablespoons rice wine vinegar
2 tablespoons lemon juice
2 tablespoons honey
2 teaspoons cornstarch
1 teaspoon reduced-sodium soy sauce
½ teaspoon ground ginger
1 pound skinless boneless chicken
  thighs or breast halves, cut into thin
  slices
1 cup thinly sliced green bell pepper
  (about 1 medium)
½ cup thinly sliced red bell pepper
  (about 1 small)
½ cup thinly sliced yellow bell pepper
  (about 1 small)
¼ cup 1-inch pieces green onion (2 to 3
  medium)
2 cups hot cooked brown or white rice

Mix pineapple juice, vinegar, lemon juice, honey, cornstarch, soy sauce and ginger; reserve.

Spray wok or 12-inch nonstick skillet with nonstick cooking spray. Heat until hot. Add chicken, bell peppers and onion; stir-fry about 5 minutes or until chicken is white and peppers are crisp-tender. Add reserved pineapple juice mixture; stir-fry about 2 minutes or until mixture is thickened and bubbly. Serve over rice.

4 servings

PER SERVING: Calories 295; Protein 19 g; Carbohydrate 41 g; Fat 6 g; Cholesterol 50 mg; Sodium 380 mg

Chicken Almond Ding

Our microwave do-ahead tip lets you get a jump on dinner when you know your schedule is hectic.

2 whole chicken breasts (about 2
   pounds)
1 egg white
1 teaspoon cornstarch
½ teaspoon salt
Dash of white pepper
1 teaspoon soy sauce
2 medium carrots
2 tablespoons oyster sauce or 1 tablespoon soy sauce
1 tablespoon plus 1 teaspoon cornstarch
¼ teaspoon water
Vegetable oil
2 tablespoons vegetable oil
¼ cup diced onion (about 1 small)
1 teaspoon finely chopped garlic
1 teaspoon finely chopped gingerroot
1 cup diced celery
½ cup diced canned water chestnuts
½ teaspoon salt
½ cup diced bamboo shoots
1 can (4 ounces) button mushrooms,
   drained
½ cup chicken broth
1 cup frozen peas
½ cup roasted whole almonds
2 tablespoons chopped green onions
   (with tops)

Remove skin and bones from chicken; cut chicken into ½-inch pieces. Mix egg white, 1 teaspoon cornstarch, ½ teaspoon salt, the white pepper and soy sauce in glass or plastic bowl; stir in chicken. Cover and refrigerate 30 minutes.

Cut carrots into ½-inch pieces. Place carrots in boiling water. Cover and cook 1 minute. Immediately rinse under running cold water; drain. Mix oyster sauce, 1 tablespoon plus 1 teaspoon cornstarch and the water.

Heat vegetable oil (1 inch) in wok to 325°. Add chicken; fry, turning frequently, until chicken turns white. Remove from wok to strainer. Wash and dry wok thoroughly.

Heat wok until 1 or 2 drops of water bubble and skitter when sprinkled in wok. Add 2 tablespoons vegetable oil; rotate wok to coat side. Add onion, garlic and gingerroot; stir-fry until garlic is light brown. Add celery, water chestnuts and ½ teaspoon salt; stir-fry 1 minute. Add bamboo shoots and mushrooms; stir-fry 1 minute. Stir in carrots, chicken and broth. Heat to boiling; cover and cook 2 minutes. Stir in cornstarch mixture; cook and stir until thickened, about 20 seconds. Stir in peas. Garnish with almonds and green onions. **6 servings**

MICROWAVE DO-AHEAD TIP: Prepare Chicken Almond Ding as directed—except omit peas, almonds and green onions; cover and refrigerate no longer than 24 hours. Just before serving, prepare peas, almonds and green onions. Cover chicken mixture tightly and microwave on microwavable platter or bowl on high 5 minutes; stir in peas. Cover and microwave until hot, about 5 minutes longer. Garnish with almonds and green onions.

PER SERVING: Calories 350; Protein 29 g; Carbohydrate 16 g; Fat 19 g; Cholesterol 60 mg; Sodium 990 mg

Chicken Almond Ding

Sichuan Chicken with Cashews

2 whole chicken breasts (about 2
   pounds)
1 egg white
1 teaspoon cornstarch
1 teaspoon soy sauce
Dash of white pepper
1 large green bell pepper
1 medium onion
1 can (8½ ounces) sliced bamboo
   shoots, drained
1 tablespoon cornstarch
1 tablespoon cold water
1 tablespoon soy sauce
2 tablespoons vegetable oil
1 cup raw cashews
¼ teaspoon salt
2 tablespoons vegetable oil
1 teaspoon finely chopped gingerroot
1 tablespoon hoisin sauce
2 teaspoons chile paste
¼ cup chicken broth
2 tablespoons chopped green onion

Remove skin and bones from chicken breasts; cut chicken into ¾-inch pieces. Mix egg white, 1 teaspoon cornstarch, 1 teaspoon soy sauce and the white pepper in medium glass or plastic bowl; stir in chicken. Cover and refrigerate 20 minutes.

Cut bell pepper into ¾-inch pieces. Cut onion into 8 pieces. Cut bamboo shoots into ½-inch pieces. Mix 1 tablespoon cornstarch, the water and 1 tablespoon soy sauce.

Heat wok until very hot. Add 2 tablespoons oil; tilt wok to coat side. Add cashews; stir-fry 1 minute or until cashews are light brown. Remove cashews from wok; drain on paper towel. Sprinkle with salt. Add chicken to wok; stir-fry until chicken turns white. Remove chicken from wok.

Add 2 tablespoons oil; tilt wok to coat side. Add onion pieces and gingerroot; stir-fry until gingerroot is light brown. Add chicken, bell pepper, bamboo shoots, hoisin sauce and chile paste; stir-fry 1 minute. Add broth; heat to boiling. Stir in cornstarch mixture; cook and stir 20 seconds or until thickened. Stir in cashews and onion. **4 servings**

PER SERVING: Calories 570; Protein 44 g; Carbohydrate 20 g; Fat 35 g; Cholesterol 90 mg; Sodium 830 mg

Chicken with Almonds

1 tablespoon vegetable oil
6 skinless boneless chicken breast
   halves (about 1½ pounds), cut into 1-
   inch pieces
1 can (8 ounces) sliced water chestnuts,
   drained
1 can (8 ounces) sliced bamboo shoots,
   drained
¾ cup sliced celery (about 1 large stalk)
¾ cup sliced mushrooms (about 2
   ounces)
¾ cup chicken broth
2 teaspoons reduced-sodium soy sauce
2 tablespoons cornstarch
2 tablespoons cold water
2 tablespoons sliced almonds

Heat oil in wok or 12-inch nonstick skillet until hot. Add chicken; stir-fry over high heat about 5 minutes or until white. Reduce heat to medium. Add water chestnuts, bamboo shoots, celery and mushrooms; stir-fry over high heat 3 to 5 minutes or until heated through. Stir in broth and soy sauce. Heat to boiling; reduce heat. Cover and simmer 6 minutes.

Mix cornstarch and cold water; stir into chicken mixture. Cook and stir about 30 seconds or until thickened. Sprinkle with almonds.

6 servings

PER SERVING: Calories 220; Protein 28 g; Carbohydrate 11 g; Fat 7 g; Cholesterol 65 mg; Sodium 250 mg

Sichuan Chicken with Cashews

Walnut Chicken

2 cups water
1 cup walnuts
¼ teaspoon sugar
2 whole chicken breasts (about 2
    pounds)
1 egg white
2 teaspoons cornstarch
1 teaspoon salt
⅛ teaspoon white pepper
2 ounces Chinese pea pods
2 stalks celery
2 green onions (with tops)
2 tablespoons oyster sauce
1 tablespoon cornstarch
1 tablespoon water
1 cup vegetable oil
½ cup chicken broth
1 tablespoon diced pimiento

Heat 2 cups water to boiling; add walnuts. Heat to boiling; boil 1 minute. Drain; rinse under cold water. Remove skin from walnuts; sprinkle walnuts with sugar.

Remove skin and bones from chicken breasts; cut chicken into ¾-inch pieces. Mix egg white, 2 teaspoons cornstarch, the salt and white pepper in medium bowl; stir in chicken. Cover and refrigerate 20 minutes.

Remove strings from pea pods; cut large pea pods into 3 pieces. Place pea pods in boiling water; heat to boiling. Boil 30 seconds; drain. Immediately rinse in cold water. Cut celery diagonally into ¼-inch slices. Cut green onions diagonally into 1-inch pieces. Mix oyster sauce, 1 tablespoon cornstarch and 1 tablespoon water.

Heat oil in wok to 350°. Add walnuts; fry until walnuts are light brown. Remove walnuts from oil, using slotted spoon; drain on paper towels.

Add chicken; fry until chicken turns white, stirring to separate pieces. Remove chicken from oil, using slotted spoon; drain on paper towels. Pour oil from wok, reserving 2 tablespoons.

Heat wok until very hot. Add 2 tablespoons reserved oil; tilt wok to coat side. Add celery; stir-fry 1 minute. Add broth; heat to boiling. Cover and simmer 1 minute. Add chicken, pea pods, green onions and pimiento; heat to boiling. Stir in cornstarch mixture; cook and stir until mixture thickens. Stir in walnuts. **4 servings**

PER SERVING: Calories 520; Protein 42 g; Carbohydrate 12 g; Fat 34 g; Cholesterol 90 mg; Sodium 1090 mg

Chicken and Egg Stir-fry

1 whole chicken breast (about 1 pound)
½ teaspoon cornstarch
½ teaspoon salt
2 tablespoons vegetable oil
½ cup frozen peas
6 eggs, slightly beaten
¼ cup chopped green onions (with tops)
½ teaspoon salt
Dash of white pepper

Remove skin and bones from chicken; cut chicken into ½-inch pieces. Toss chicken, cornstarch and ½ teaspoon salt.

Heat wok until 1 or 2 drops of water bubble and skitter when sprinkled in wok. Add oil; rotate wok to coat side. Add chicken; stir-fry until chicken turns white. Add peas; stir-fry 1 minute. Reduce heat to medium.

Mix eggs, green onions, ½ teaspoon salt and the white pepper; pour into wok. Cook and stir until eggs are thickened throughout but still moist, about 2 minutes. **4 servings**

PER SERVING: Calories 280; Protein 28 g; Carbohydrate 4 g; Fat 17 g; Cholesterol 360 mg; Sodium 680 mg

Shredded Chicken with Bean Sprouts and Pea Pods

Take care not to overcook the sprouts in this recipe or they will become soggy and limp. Briefly stir-fried, they'll stay plump and crisp.

2 whole chicken breasts (about 2 pounds)
1 teaspoon cornstarch
½ teaspoon salt
⅛ teaspoon white pepper
4 ounces Chinese pea pods
1 pound bean sprouts
2 tablespoons chicken broth
1 tablespoon dark soy sauce
2 teaspoons cornstarch
1 teaspoon sugar
1 tablespoon vegetable oil
½ teaspoon salt
2 tablespoons vegetable oil
2 teaspoons finely chopped garlic
1 teaspoon finely chopped gingerroot
¼ cup chicken broth

Remove skin and bones from chicken breasts; cut chicken into 2 × ½-inch pieces. Stack slices; cut into thin strips. Toss chicken, 1 teaspoon cornstarch, ½ teaspoon salt and the white pepper in medium bowl. Cover and refrigerate 30 minutes.

Remove strings from pea pods. Place pea pods in boiling water; heat to boiling. Immediately remove from heat; drain. Immediately rinse in cold water; drain. Rinse bean sprouts in cold water; drain thoroughly. Mix 2 tablespoons broth, the soy sauce, 2 teaspoons cornstarch and the sugar.

Heat wok until very hot. Add 1 tablespoon oil; tilt wok to coat side. Add bean sprouts and ½ teaspoon salt; stir-fry 2 minutes. Remove bean sprouts from wok; drain.

Heat wok until very hot. Add 2 tablespoons oil; tilt wok to coat side. Add chicken, garlic and gingerroot; stir-fry 2 minutes or until chicken turns white. Add bean sprouts and pea pods; stir-fry 1 minute. Add ¼ cup broth; heat to boiling. Stir in cornstarch mixture; cook and stir until thickened. **4 servings**

PER SERVING: Calories 490; Protein 52 g; Carbohydrate 19 g; Fat 23 g; Cholesterol 90 mg; Sodium 960 mg

Buying Chicken

Selecting fresh, wholesome poultry is easy if you follow these guidelines:

- Package trays or bags should have very little or no liquid in the bottom.
- Avoid torn and leaking packages.
- Avoid packages that are stacked in the refrigerator case too high; these packages are not being kept cool enough, which shortens shelf-life.
- Frozen chicken should be firm to the touch and free of freezer burn and tears in packaging.
- Boneless, skinless products should look plump and moist.
- The color of chicken skin doesn't indicate quality. Skin color ranges from yellow to white depending on what the chicken was fed.
- The cut ends of the chicken bones should be pink to red in color, if they are gray, the chicken is not as fresh.

Chicken-Chutney Stir-fry

Stir-fried Chicken with Cucumbers

Chicken breasts can be used instead of the thighs. You will need 2 whole chicken breasts (about 2 pounds). To remove bones from chicken thighs, cut down the center of the thigh to the bone; separate the meat from the bone.

6 chicken thighs (about 1 pound)
1 tablespoon cornstarch
½ teaspoon salt
⅛ teaspoon white pepper
6 medium dried black mushrooms
1 medium cucumber
6 green onions (with tops)
1 tablespoon dry white wine
1 tablespoon soy sauce
1 teaspoon sugar
1 teaspoon cornstarch
3 tablespoons vegetable oil
1 teaspoon finely chopped gingerroot
1 teaspoon finely chopped garlic

Remove skin and bones from chicken thighs; cut chicken into 1 × ½-inch pieces. Toss chicken, 1 tablespoon cornstarch, the salt and white pepper in medium bowl. Cover and refrigerate 20 minutes.

Soak mushrooms in hot water 20 minutes or until soft; drain. Rinse in warm water; drain. Squeeze out excess moisture. Remove and discard stems; cut caps into ¼-inch slices. Pare cucumber; cut lengthwise into halves. Remove seeds; cut cucumber diagonally into ¼-inch-thick slices. Cut green onions diagonally into 1-inch pieces. Mix wine, soy sauce, sugar and 1 teaspoon cornstarch.

Heat wok until very hot. Add oil; tilt wok to coat side. Add chicken, mushrooms, gingerroot and garlic; stir-fry 2 minutes, separating chicken pieces. Add cucumber; stir-fry 1 minute. Add green onions and soy sauce mixture; cook and stir 1 minute. **4 servings**

PER SERVING: Calories 235; Protein 17 g; Carbohydrate 8 g; Fat 15 g; Cholesterol 50 mg; Sodium 580 mg

Chicken-Chutney Stir-fry

1 tablespoon vegetable oil
3 skinless boneless chicken breast halves (about 1 pound), cut into 1-inch pieces
2 carrots, thinly sliced (about 1 cup)
½ medium red bell pepper, cut into thin strips
1 tablespoon cornstarch
1 tablespoon soy sauce
½ cup chutney
6 ounces pea pods
¼ cup chopped peanuts

Heat oil in 10-inch skillet or wok until hot. Add chicken, carrots and bell pepper. Stir-fry over medium-high heat 5 to 7 minutes or until chicken is white. Mix cornstarch, soy sauce and chutney. Stir into chicken mixture. Cook and stir over medium heat until slightly thickened. Stir in pea pods; heat until hot. Serve over rice if desired. Sprinkle with peanuts.

PER SERVING: Calories 305; Protein 29 g; Carbohydrate 22 g; Fat 11 g; Cholesterol 60 mg; Sodium 360 mg

Curried Chicken and Nectarines

Curried Chicken and Nectarines

Curry and nectarines combine for an unusual—and tasty—stir-fry.

4 boneless skinless chicken breast halves (about 1 pound)
2 tablespoons reduced-calorie oil-and-vinegar dressing
1 teaspoon curry powder
¼ cup raisins
¼ cup sliced green onions (with tops)
¼ teaspoon salt
1 medium bell pepper, cut into ¼-inch strips
2 small nectarines, cut into ¼-inch slices

Trim fat from chicken breast halves. Cut chicken crosswise into ½-inch strips. Mix dressing and curry powder in medium bowl. Add chicken; toss. Heat 10-inch nonstick skillet over medium-high heat. Stir in chicken and remaining ingredients except nectarines; stir-fry 4 to 6 minutes or until chicken is done. Stir in nectarines carefully; heat through. Serve with hot cooked rice or couscous if desired. **4 servings**

MICROWAVE DIRECTIONS: Prepare chicken as directed. Mix dressing and curry powder in 2-quart microwavable casserole. Add chicken; toss. Stir in remaining ingredients except nectarines. Cover tightly and microwave on high 8 to 10 minutes, stirring after 4 minutes, until chicken is done. Stir in nectarines carefully. Cover and microwave 1 minute or until heated through.

PER SERVING: Calories 210; Protein 25 g; Carbohydrate 15 g; Fat 6 g; Cholesterol 80 mg; Sodium 230 mg

Italian Chicken Stir-fry

Pepperoni cut into strips rather than left in slices makes that marvelous flavor go further.

1 pound skinless boneless chicken breasts
1 tablespoon olive or vegetable oil
¼ cup ¼-inch strips thinly sliced pepperoni (about 1 ounce)
2 cloves garlic, finely chopped
2 large bell peppers, cut into 1-inch squares
1 medium onion, thinly sliced
2 cups ¼-inch zucchini slices (about 2 medium)
¼ cup dry red wine
1 teaspoon chopped fresh or ½ teaspoon dried thyme leaves
1 teaspoon chopped fresh or ½ teaspoon dried rosemary leaves
¼ teaspoon salt
⅛ teaspoon pepper
1 tablespoon grated Parmesan cheese

Remove excess fat from chicken; cut chicken into 2-inch pieces. Heat oil in 10-inch nonstick skillet or wok over medium-high heat. Add chicken, pepperoni and garlic; stir-fry until chicken is almost done, 3 to 4 minutes. Remove chicken mixture from skillet; keep warm.

Heat remaining ingredients except cheese to boiling in skillet; stir-fry until vegetables are crisp-tender, 3 to 4 minutes. Stir in chicken mixture; heat through. Sprinkle with Parmesan cheese. **4 servings**

PER SERVING: Calories 290; Protein 37 g; Carbohydrate 10 g; Fat 10 g; Cholesterol 95 mg; Sodium 370 mg

Sesame Chicken with Fun See

A Chinese saying claims that sesame seed improves the spirits; it assuredly improves flavors! The quickly fried cellophane noodles here (fun see) *add crunch to this hot-and-sour dish.*

2 whole chicken breasts (about 2 pounds)
1 egg
2 tablespoons all-purpose flour
2 tablespoons cornstarch
2 tablespoons water
1 teaspoon salt
2 teaspoons vegetable oil
¼ teaspoon baking soda
¼ teaspoon white pepper
½ cup water
¼ cup cornstarch
1 cup sugar
1 cup chicken broth
¾ cup vinegar
2 teaspoons dark soy sauce
2 teaspoons chile paste
1 teaspoon vegetable oil
1 clove garlic, finely chopped
Vegetable oil
2 ounces rice stick noodles
2 tablespoons toasted sesame seed

Remove skin and bones from chicken breasts; cut chicken into 2 × ½-inch strips. Mix egg, flour, 2 tablespoons cornstarch, 2 tablespoons water, the salt, 2 teaspoons oil, the baking soda and white pepper; stir in chicken. Cover and refrigerate 20 minutes. Mix ½ cup water and ¼ cup cornstarch.

Heat sugar, broth, vinegar, soy sauce, chile paste, 1 teaspoon oil and the garlic to boiling. Stir in cornstarch mixture; cook and stir until thickened. Remove from heat; keep warm.

Heat oil (1½ inches) in wok to 350°. Pull noodles apart gently. Fry ¼ of the noodles at a time 5 seconds or until puffed, turning once; drain on paper towels.

Heat oil to 350°. Fry about 10 pieces of chicken, adding 1 at a time, 3 minutes or until light brown. Remove from oil, using slotted spoon; drain on paper towels. Repeat with remaining chicken.

Heat oil to 375°. Fry about ⅓ of the chicken 1 minute or until golden brown. Remove from oil, using slotted spoon; drain on paper towels. Repeat with remaining chicken. Place chicken on heated platter.

Heat sauce to boiling; pour over chicken. Sprinkle with sesame seed. Arrange rice stick noodles around chicken. **6 servings**

PER SERVING: Calories 450; Protein 26 g; Carbohydrate 51 g; Fat 16 g; Cholesterol 60 mg; Sodium 720 mg

Sesame Chicken with Fun See

Wings with Black Beans

8 chicken wings
3 tablespoons salted black beans
2 green onions (with tops)
2 tablespoons vegetable oil
1 teaspoon finely shredded gingerroot
1 teaspoon finely chopped garlic
1 tablespoon dry white wine
2 teaspoons dark soy sauce
1 teaspoon sugar
¾ cup chicken broth
1 tablespoon cornstarch
1 tablespoon cold water

Cut each chicken wing at joints to make 3 pieces. Discard tips. Soak beans in warm water 15 minutes. Rinse in cold water to remove skins; drain. Mash beans. Cut green onions into 2-inch pieces.

Heat wok until 2 drops of water bubble and skitter when sprinkled in wok. Add oil; rotate wok to coat. Add chicken, gingerroot and garlic; stir-fry 2 minutes. Add beans; stir-fry 1 minute. Stir in wine, soy sauce and sugar; stir to coat chicken. Stir in broth; heat to boiling. Reduce heat; cover and simmer 15 minutes.

Mix cornstarch and water; stir into chicken mixture. Cook and stir until thickened, about 10 seconds. Garnish with green onions.

4 servings

PER SERVING: Calories 295; Protein 19 g; Carbohydrate 5 g; Fat 22 g; Cholesterol 60 mg; Sodium 470 mg

Wings with Oyster Sauce

8 chicken wings
2 green onions (with tops)
3 tablespoons vegetable oil
1 teaspoon finely chopped gingerroot
1 teaspoon finely chopped garlic
¼ cup oyster sauce
1 tablespoon dry white wine
1 teaspoon dark soy sauce
¾ cup chicken broth
1 tablespoon cornstarch
1 tablespoon cold water

Cut each chicken wing at joints to make 3 pieces. Cut green onions into 2-inch pieces.

Heat wok until 1 or 2 drops of water bubble and skitter when sprinkled in wok. Add oil; rotate wok to coat. Add chicken, gingerroot and garlic; stir-fry 2 minutes.

Stir in oyster sauce, wine and soy sauce; stir to coat chicken. Stir in broth; heat to boiling. Reduce heat; cover and simmer 15 minutes.

Mix cornstarch and water; stir into chicken mixture. Cook and stir until thickened, about 10 seconds. Garnish with green onions.

4 servings

MICROWAVE REHEAT DIRECTIONS: Prepare Chicken Wings with Oyster Sauce as directed—except omit green onions; cover and refrigerate no longer than 24 hours. Just before serving, prepare green onions. Cover chicken mixture tightly and microwave on microwaveproof platter or bowl on high 4 minutes; turn chicken. Cover and microwave until hot, about 3 minutes longer. Let stand covered 2 minutes. Garnish with green onions.

PER SERVING: Calories 330; Protein 20 g; Carbohydrate 6 g; Fat 25 g; Cholesterol 60 mg; Sodium 970 mg

Lemon Rice with Turkey

Brown rice has a hearty flavor that blends well with lemon. You may want to decrease the lemon juice to ¼ cup if using white rice.

- 1 cup chopped green onions (about 9 medium)
- 1 cup chicken broth
- 2 cloves garlic, finely chopped
- 1½-pound turkey breast, cut into 3 × ¼ × ¼-inch strips
- 3 cups cooked brown or white rice
- ⅓ cup lemon juice
- 1 tablespoon capers, rinsed and drained
- 2 teaspoons grated lemon peel
- ¼ teaspoon pepper
- 3 tablespoons chopped fresh parsley

Cook onions, broth and garlic in 12-inch skillet over medium heat 3 minutes, stirring occasionally, until onions are tender. Stir in turkey. Cook 3 minutes. Stir in remaining ingredients except parsley. Cook about 3 minutes or until rice is hot and turkey is white; remove from heat. Stir in parsley. **6 servings**

PER SERVING: Calories 265; Protein 30 g; Carbohydrate 25 g; Fat 5 g; Cholesterol 65 mg; Sodium 200 mg

Turkey and Vegetable Stir-fry

- 1 cup chopped broccoli
- ⅓ cup chopped onion
- 2 cloves garlic, finely chopped
- 1 medium carrot, cut into julienne strips
- 1 tablespoon vegetable oil
- 2 cups cut-up cooked turkey or chicken
- 1 teaspoon salt
- 2 cups chopped tomatoes (about 2 medium)
- 4 cups hot cooked spaghetti or fettuccine
- ⅓ cup freshly grated Parmesan cheese
- 2 tablespoons chopped fresh parsley

Cook and stir broccoli, onion, garlic and carrot in oil in 10-inch nonstick skillet over medium heat until broccoli is crisp-tender, about 10 minutes. Stir in turkey, salt and tomatoes; heat just until turkey is hot, about 3 minutes. Spoon turkey mixture over spaghetti; sprinkle with cheese and parsley. **6 servings**

PER SERVING: Calories 235; Protein 19 g; Carbohydrate 26 g; Fat 6 g; Cholesterol 40 mg; Sodium 490 mg

Halibut with Salted Black Beans and Chiles

3

Fish & Seafood

Halibut with Salted Black Beans and Chiles

Chinese recipes for fin fish—no matter what kind—always include gingerroot. This halibut is coated with it and then is given even more flavor with the addition of garlic, hot green chiles and black beans.

1 pound halibut steak
1 teaspoon salt
1 teaspoon finely chopped gingerroot
¼ teaspoon white pepper
1 teaspoon cornstarch
2 tablespoons salted black beans
4 green onions (with tops)
2 hot green chiles
1 tablespoon cornstarch
1 tablespoon water
1 teaspoon sugar
2 tablespoons vegetable oil
1 tablespoon vegetable oil
2 teaspoons finely chopped garlic
1 cup chicken broth
Spinach or lettuce leaves

Pat fish dry with paper towels. Mix salt, gingerroot and white pepper. Coat both sides of fish with gingerroot mixture. Rub 1 teaspoon cornstarch on both sides of fish. Cover and refrigerate 30 minutes.

Place beans in bowl; cover with warm water. Stir beans about 2 minutes to remove excess salt. Remove beans from water; drain well.

Cut 3 green onions diagonally into 1-inch pieces. Cut remaining green onion into thin slices. Remove seeds and membranes from chiles. Cut chiles into very thin slices. Mix 1 tablespoon cornstarch, the water and sugar.

Heat wok over medium heat until hot. Add 2 tablespoons oil; tilt wok to coat side. Fry fish 2 minutes or until brown, turning once. Reduce heat to low; cover and simmer 10 minutes, turning after 3 minutes. Remove fish from wok.

Heat wok until very hot. Add 1 tablespoon oil; tilt wok to coat side. Add beans, chiles, garlic and green onion pieces; stir-fry 1 minute. Add broth; heat to boiling. Stir in cornstarch mixture; cook and stir until thickened. Add fish; turn fish to coat with sauce. Heat 2 minutes. Line serving platter with spinach leaves. Place fish on spinach; sprinkle with green onion slices.

4 servings

PER SERVING: Calories 235; Protein 24 g; Carbohydrate 8 g; Fat 12 g; Cholesterol 60 mg; Sodium 900 mg

Halibut Stir-fry

Sesame oil with its high smoking point is perfect for a stir-fry. We suggest using darker, Asian sesame oil in this recipe as it has a more robust flavor than light sesame oil.

2 teaspoons sesame oil
1 pound halibut or other lean fish steaks, cut into 1-inch pieces
1 medium onion, thinly sliced
3 cloves garlic, finely chopped
1 teaspoon finely chopped gingerroot
1 package (10 ounces) frozen asparagus cuts, thawed and drained
1 cup sliced mushrooms (about 3 ounces) or 1 can (4 ounces) sliced mushrooms, drained
1 medium tomato, cut into thin wedges
2 tablespoons soy sauce
1 tablespoon lemon juice

Heat oil in 10-inch nonstick skillet over medium-high heat. Add fish, onion, garlic, gingerroot and asparagus; stir-fry 2 to 3 minutes or until fish almost flakes with fork. Carefully stir in remaining ingredients; heat thoroughly. Serve with additional soy sauce if desired. **4 servings**

PER SERVING: Calories 195; Protein 27 g; Carbohydrate 10 g; Fat 5 g; Cholesterol 35 mg; Sodium 730 mg

Stir-fried Fish with Pea Pods

1 pound walleye fillets
1 tablespoon vegetable oil
1 teaspoon cornstarch
1 teaspoon salt
1 teaspoon light soy sauce
¼ teaspoon sesame oil
⅛ teaspoon white pepper
8 ounces pea pods
3 green onions (with tops)
3 tablespoons vegetable oil
1 clove garlic, finely chopped
1 teaspoon finely chopped gingerroot
2 tablespoons oyster sauce

Cut fish into strips, 2 × 1 inch. Toss fish strips, 1 tablespoon oil, the cornstarch, salt, soy sauce, sesame oil and white pepper in glass or plastic bowl. Cover and refrigerate 30 minutes. Remove strings from pea pods. Place pea pods in boiling water. Cover and cook 1 minute; drain. Immediately rinse under running cold water; drain. Cut green onions into 2-inch pieces.

Heat wok until 1 or 2 drops of water bubble and skitter when sprinkled in wok. Add 3 tablespoons oil; rotate wok to coat side. Add fish, garlic and gingerroot; stir-fry until fish turns white. Add pea pods and green onions; stir-fry 1 minute. Stir oyster sauce into mixture. **4 servings**

PER SERVING: Calories 265; Protein 25 g; Carbohydrate 7 g; Fat 15 g; Cholesterol 60 mg; Sodium 1060 mg

Stir-fried Fish with Vegetables

1 pound walleye or sea bass fillets
1½ teaspoons vegetable oil
1 teaspoon cornstarch
½ teaspoon salt
½ teaspoon light soy sauce
⅛ teaspoon white pepper
⅛ teaspoon sesame oil
1 pound bok choy (about 7 large stalks)
6 ounces pea pods
4 ounces mushrooms
2 green onions (with tops)
2 tablespoons cornstarch
2 tablespoons cold water
¼ cup vegetable oil
1 teaspoon finely chopped gingerroot
1 teaspoon finely chopped garlic
2 tablespoons vegetable oil
2 tablespoons oyster sauce or 1 table-spoon dark soy sauce
1 teaspoon salt
½ cup chicken broth

Cut fish across grain into ½-inch strips. Toss fish strips, 1½ teaspoons vegetable oil, 1 teaspoon cornstarch, ½ teaspoon salt, the soy sauce, white pepper and sesame oil in glass or plastic bowl. Cover and refrigerate 30 minutes.

Separate bok choy leaves from stems. Cut leaves into 2-inch pieces; cut stems diagonally into ¼-inch slices (do not combine leaves and stems). Remove strings from pea pods. Place pea pods in boiling water. Cover and cook 1 minute; drain. Immediately rinse under running cold water; drain. Cut mushrooms into ½-inch slices. Cut green onions into 2-inch pieces. Mix 2 tablespoons cornstarch and the water.

Heat wok until 1 or 2 drops of water bubble and skitter when sprinkled in wok. Add ¼ cup vegetable oil; rotate wok to coat side. Add gingerroot and garlic; stir-fry until light brown. Add fish; stir-fry until fish turns white. Remove fish from wok.

Add 2 tablespoons vegetable oil to wok; rotate to coat side. Add bok choy stems and mushrooms; stir-fry 1 minute. Stir in bok choy leaves, oyster sauce and 1 teaspoon salt. Stir in broth; heat to boiling. Stir in cornstarch mixture; cook and stir until thickened. Add fish and pea pods; stir-fry 1 minute. Garnish fish with green onions. **6 servings**

PER SERVING: Calories 250; Protein 18 g; Carbohydrate 8 g; Fat 16 g; Cholesterol 40 mg; Sodium 940 mg

---

Fish Tips

Selecting Fresh Fish
- Eyes should be bright, clear and not sunken.
- Gills should be reddish pink, never brown.
- Scales should be bright with a sheen.
- Flesh should be firm and elastic; it should spring back when touched.
- There should be no odor.

Selecting Frozen Fish
- Package should be tightly wrapped and frozen solid with little or no airspace between package and fish.
- There should be no discoloration; if the fish is discolored, this may indicate freezer burn.
- There should be no odor.

Stir-fried Walleye with Celery Cabbage

½ pound walleye or sea bass fillets
1 teaspoon cornstarch
1 teaspoon vegetable oil
½ teaspoon salt
½ teaspoon finely chopped gingerroot
Dash of white pepper
10 ounces celery cabbage
2 green onions (with tops)
1 tablespoon cornstarch
1 tablespoon water
3 tablespoons vegetable oil
1 teaspoon salt
1 teaspoon finely chopped garlic
¼ cup chicken broth
1 teaspoon soy sauce
¼ teaspoon roasted sesame oil

Pat fish dry with paper towels. Cut fish crosswise into 1-inch pieces. Toss fish, 1 teaspoon cornstarch, 1 teaspoon vegetable oil, ½ teaspoon salt, the gingerroot and white pepper in medium bowl. Cover and refrigerate 30 minutes.

Cut celery cabbage into ½-inch slices. Cut green onions diagonally into 2-inch pieces. Mix 1 tablespoon cornstarch and the water.

Heat wok until very hot. Add 3 tablespoons vegetable oil; tilt wok to coat side. Add fish; stir-fry gently 2 minutes or until fish turns white. Remove fish from wok.

Add 1 teaspoon salt, the garlic and celery cabbage; stir-fry 1 minute. Add broth; heat to boiling. Add cornstarch mixture; cook and stir until thickened. Stir in fish, green onions, soy sauce, and sesame oil; cook and stir 1 minute or until fish is hot. **4 servings**

PER SERVING: Calories 185; Protein 12 g; Carbohydrate 5 g; Fat 13 g; Cholesterol 30 mg; Sodium 990 mg

Sea Bass with Green Beans

½ pound sea bass or walleye fillets
1 teaspoon cornstarch
1 teaspoon roasted sesame oil
½ teaspoon salt
½ teaspoon finely chopped gingerroot
Dash of white pepper
10 ounces green beans
1 green onion (with top)
1 tablespoon cornstarch
1 tablespoon water
1 teaspoon sugar
¼ teaspoon roasted sesame oil
2 tablespoons vegetable oil
2 tablespoons vegetable oil
1 teaspoon finely chopped garlic
½ teaspoon salt
½ cup chicken broth

Pat fish dry with paper towels. Cut fish into 2 × ½-inch slices. Toss fish, 1 teaspoon cornstarch, 1 teaspoon sesame oil, ½ teaspoon salt, the gingerroot and white pepper in medium bowl. Cover and refrigerate 20 minutes. Snap green beans into halves. Cut green onion diagonally into 1-inch pieces. Mix 1 tablespoon cornstarch and the water. Mix sugar and ¼ teaspoon sesame oil.

Heat wok until very hot. Add 2 tablespoons vegetable oil; tilt wok to coat side. Add fish; stir-fry gently 2 minutes or until fish turns white. Remove fish from wok.

Heat wok until very hot. Add 2 tablespoons vegetable oil; tilt wok to coat side. Add green beans, garlic and ½ teaspoon salt; stir-fry 1 minute. Add broth; heat to boiling. Cover and cook 2 minutes. Stir in cornstarch mixture; cook and stir until mixture thickens. Add fish and onion; cook and stir gently 30 seconds. Gently stir in sesame oil mixture. **4 servings**

PER SERVING: Calories 225; Protein 12 g; Carbohydrate 8 g; Fat 16 g; Cholesterol 30 mg; Sodium 690 mg

Sea Bass with Green Beans

Scallops with Broccoli and Mushrooms

1 pound scallops
4 ounces mushrooms, sliced (about 1½ cups)
2 tablespoons margarine or butter
2 cups cut-up broccoli or 1 package (10 ounces) frozen chopped broccoli, thawed
1 jar (2 ounces) sliced pimientos, drained
1 can (10¾ ounces) condensed chicken broth
3 tablespoons cornstarch
2 teaspoons soy sauce
Hot cooked rice or pasta

If scallops are large, cut into halves. Cook and stir mushrooms in margarine in 3-quart sauce-pan over medium heat until tender, about 5 minutes. Stir in scallops, broccoli and pimientos. Cook, stirring frequently, until scallops are white, 3 to 4 minutes.

Gradually stir broth into cornstarch until smooth. Stir broth mixture and soy sauce into scallop mixture. Heat to boiling, stirring constantly. Boil and stir 1 minute. Serve over rice.

4 servings

PER SERVING: Calories 400; Protein 35 g; Carbohydrate 45 g; Fat 9 g; Cholesterol 35 mg; Sodium 1440 mg

Stir-fried Scallops and Pea Pods

Bacon adds a pleasant, unexpected flavor to the scallops and pea pods.

1 pound scallops
1 tablespoon packed brown sugar
1 tablespoon soy sauce
2 teaspoons cornstarch
6 slices bacon, cut into 1-inch pieces
6 green onions (with tops), cut into 1-inch pieces
1 can (8 ounces) sliced water chestnuts, drained
4 ounces fresh Chinese pea pods or 1 package (6 ounces) frozen Chinese pea pods, thawed

If scallops are large, cut into halves. Toss scallops, brown sugar, soy sauce and cornstarch in bowl; cover and refrigerate 10 minutes.

Cook and stir bacon in 10-inch skillet or wok over medium heat until crisp. Drain, reserving 1 tablespoon fat in skillet; reserve bacon.

Cook and stir scallops, onions and water chestnuts in bacon fat over medium-high heat until scallops are white, about 7 minutes; stir in pea pods. Stir in bacon just before serving.

4 servings

PER SERVING: Calories 275; Protein 30 g; Carbohydrate 19 g; Fat 9 g; Cholesterol 45 mg; Sodium 750 mg

Stir-fried Scallops and Pea Pods

Stir-fried Shrimp

1 pound fresh or frozen raw shrimp
1 teaspoon cornstarch
1 teaspoon dry white wine
¼ teaspoon salt
¼ teaspoon sesame oil
2 tablespoons salted black beans
1 tablespoon cornstarch
¼ cup chicken broth
1 teaspoon dark soy sauce
1 tablespoon vegetable oil
½ pound ground pork
2 tablespoons vegetable oil
2 cloves garlic, finely chopped
1 teaspoon finely chopped gingerroot
¼ cup chicken broth
2 tablespoons dry white wine
2 eggs, slightly beaten
2 green onions (with tops), chopped

Peel shrimp. (If shrimp are frozen, do not thaw; peel under running cold water.) Make a shallow cut lengthwise down back of each shrimp; wash out sand vein. Toss shrimp, 1 teaspoon cornstarch, 1 teaspoon wine, the salt and sesame oil in glass or plastic bowl. Cover and refrigerate 20 minutes. Soak beans in warm water 15 minutes; drain. Rinse beans in cold water to remove skins; drain. Mash beans. Mix 1 tablespoon cornstarch, ¼ cup broth and the soy sauce.

Heat wok until 1 or 2 drops of water skitter when sprinkled in wok. Add 1 tablespoon vegetable oil; rotate wok to coat side. Add pork; stir-fry until pork is no longer pink. Remove and drain. Wash and dry wok thoroughly.

Heat wok until 1 or 2 drops of water bubble and skitter when sprinkled in wok. Add 2 tablespoons vegetable oil; rotate wok to coat side. Add shrimp, mashed beans, garlic and gingerroot; stir-fry 1 minute. Stir in pork, ¼ cup broth and 2 tablespoons wine; heat to boiling. Stir in cornstarch mixture; heat to boiling. Stir in eggs. Re-move from heat; cover and let stand 30 seconds. Sprinkle with chopped green onions. **6 servings**

PER SERVING: Calories 235; Protein 17 g; Carbohydrate 3 g; Fat 17 g; Cholesterol 170 mg; Sodium 370 mg

Stir-fried Garlic Shrimp

This is an especially speedy stir-fry, and if you'd like to make it even more so, buy presliced mushrooms at a salad bar.

2 large cloves garlic, finely chopped
2 teaspoons vegetable oil
1 pound frozen peeled and deveined raw medium shrimp, thawed
3 cups sliced fresh mushrooms (about 8 ounces)
1 cup 1-inch pieces green onions (with tops)
¼ cup dry white wine
2 cups hot cooked rice

Cook garlic in oil in 10-inch nonstick skillet over medium-high heat 1 minute, stirring frequently. Add shrimp; stir-fry 1 minute. Stir in mushrooms, onions and wine; stir-fry about 2 minutes or until shrimp are pink and vegetables are hot. Serve over rice. **4 servings**

PER SERVING: Calories 230; Protein 16 g; Carbohydrate 30 g; Fat 5 g; Cholesterol 210 mg; Sodium 490 mg

Shrimp with Garlic Sauce

6 dried black mushrooms
½ medium head cabbage
4 green onions (with tops)
1 medium carrot
¾ pound raw medium shrimp (in shells)
1 teaspoon cornstarch
1 teaspoon water
2 tablespoons vegetable oil
2 teaspoons finely chopped garlic
2 tablespoons vegetable oil
¼ cup chicken broth
1 tablespoon chile paste

Soak mushrooms in hot water 20 minutes or until soft; drain. Rinse in warm water; drain. Squeeze out excess moisture. Remove and discard stems; cut caps into thin strips.

Cut cabbage into 2¾-inch pieces. Cut green onions diagonally into 1-inch pieces. Cut carrot diagonally into thin slices. Place carrot in boiling water; heat to boiling. Boil 1 minute; drain. Immediately rinse in cold water; drain.

Peel shrimp. Cut shrimp lengthwise into halves; wash out vein. Pat dry with paper towels. Mix cornstarch and water.

Heat wok until very hot. Add 2 tablespoons oil; tilt wok to coat side. Add shrimp and garlic; stir-fry until shrimp are pink. Remove shrimp from wok.

Heat wok until very hot. Add 2 tablespoons oil; tilt wok to coat side. Add mushrooms and cabbage; stir-fry 1 minute. Add broth; heat to boiling. Cover and cook 1 minute. Stir in cornstarch mixture; cook and stir 30 seconds or until thickened. Add shrimp, onions, carrots and chile paste. Cook and stir 30 seconds or until shrimp are hot. **4 servings**

PER SERVING: Calories 225; Protein 11 g; Carbohydrate 11 g; Fat 15 g; Cholesterol 80 mg; Sodium 220 mg

Shrimp and Zucchini

1 can (8¼ ounces) pineapple chunks, drained (reserve syrup)
1 package (12 ounces) frozen uncooked, peeled and deveined medium shrimp
1 tablespoon cornstarch
2 tablespoons cold water
3 tablespoons vegetable oil
1 clove garlic, finely chopped
1 medium onion, sliced
1 medium zucchini, cut into ¼-inch slices
1 tablespoon soy sauce
1 teaspoon sugar
¼ teaspoon ground ginger
2 medium tomatoes, cut into wedges

Add enough water to reserved pineapple syrup to measure ½ cup. Rinse frozen shrimp under running cold water to separate; drain. Mix cornstarch and water. Heat oil in 10-inch skillet over medium-high heat until hot. Cook and stir shrimp, garlic, onion and zucchini in oil until vegetables are crisp-tender, about 3 minutes. Add reserved pineapple syrup, the soy sauce, sugar and ginger. Heat to boiling; stir in cornstarch mixture. Cook and stir until thickened, about 10 seconds. Stir in pineapple and tomatoes; heat just until hot. Serve with hot cooked rice if desired. **4 servings**

PER SERVING: Calories 230; Protein 14 g; Carbohydrate 19 g; Fat 11 g; Cholesterol 120 mg; Sodium 410 mg

Shrimp Egg Foo Yung

8 ounces bean sprouts
1 cup cooked shrimp
8 eggs, slightly beaten
1 jar (4½ ounces) sliced mushrooms, drained
2 green onions (with tops), chopped
½ teaspoon salt
3 tablespoons vegetable oil
1½ cups chicken broth
1 tablespoon dark soy sauce
1 teaspoon light soy sauce
¼ teaspoon salt
Dash of white pepper
2 tablespoons cornstarch
2 tablespoons cold water

Rinse bean sprouts in cold water; drain. Cut shrimp into ½-inch pieces. Stir bean sprouts, shrimp, eggs, mushrooms, onions and ½ teaspoon salt just to blend.

Heat wok until 1 or 2 drops of water bubble and skitter when sprinkled in wok. Add oil; rotate wok to coat side. Reduce heat to medium-high. Pour ½ cup egg mixture into wok. Push cooked egg up over shrimp with broad spatula to form patty. Fry patty until set and golden brown, turning once, about 4 minutes. Repeat with remaining egg mixture. (Add oil if necessary.) Keep patties warm in 300° oven.

Heat broth, the soy sauces, ¼ teaspoon salt and the white pepper to boiling. Mix cornstarch and water; stir into broth mixture. Cook and stir until thickened, about 10 seconds; pour over patties. **6 servings**

DO-AHEAD DIRECTIONS: Fry egg patties; wrap, label and freeze no longer than 1 month. Just before serving, heat frozen patties uncovered in 375° oven until hot, about 25 minutes. Continue as directed.

PER SERVING: Calories 265; Protein 19 g; Carbohydrate 9 g; Fat 17 g; Cholesterol 320 mg; Sodium 900 mg

Emperor's Shrimp

This is an impressive and different dish.

1 head iceberg lettuce
2 green onions (with tops)
1 tablespoon cornstarch
1 tablespoon water
1 pound raw medium shrimp (in shells)
2 tablespoons vegetable oil
1 tablespoon finely chopped garlic
¼ cup ketchup
2 teaspoons light soy sauce
½ cup chicken broth
1 tablespoon dry white wine
2 teaspoons salt
1 teaspoon roasted sesame oil

Remove outer leaves from lettuce until head is about 4 inches in diameter. Remove core; cut 1-inch slice from core end of lettuce and discard. Place lettuce, cut side up, on round serving plate. Cut green onions into 2-inch pieces; shred lengthwise into fine strips. Cover with iced water; let stand 10 minutes or until strips curl. Mix cornstarch and water. Wash shrimp; pat dry with paper towels.

Heat wok until very hot. Add vegetable oil; tilt wok to coat side. Add shrimp and garlic; stir-fry 2 minutes or until shrimp are pink, turning once. Remove shrimp and oil from wok. Cool shrimp slightly. Remove shells and vein, leaving tails intact.

Add ketchup and soy sauce to wok; cook 30 seconds. Add broth; heat to boiling. Stir in cornstarch mixture, wine, salt and sesame oil; cook and stir until thickened. Add shrimp; heat until all sauce coats shrimp, stirring constantly. Hang shrimp, using wooden picks, tails down, around edges of lettuce; place green onions in center. **4 servings**

PER SERVING: Calories 175; Protein 14 g; Carbohydrate 10 g; Fat 9 g; Cholesterol 105 mg; Sodium 1650 mg

Emperor's Shrimp

Stir-fried Shrimp with Vegetables

1 pound raw medium shrimp (in shells)
1 teaspoon cornstarch
½ teaspoon salt
½ teaspoon roasted sesame oil
⅛ teaspoon white pepper
7 large stalks bok choy
6 ounces Chinese pea pods
4 ounces mushrooms
2 green onions (with tops)
2 tablespoons oyster sauce or 1 table-
spoon dark soy sauce
1 tablespoon cornstarch
1 tablespoon cold water
2 tablespoons vegetable oil
1 teaspoon finely chopped gingerroot
1 teaspoon finely chopped garlic
1 tablespoon vegetable oil
½ teaspoon salt
½ cup chicken broth

Peel shrimp. Make a shallow cut lengthwise down back of each shrimp; wash out vein. Pat dry with paper towels. Toss shrimp, 1 teaspoon cornstarch, ½ teaspoon salt, the sesame oil and white pepper in medium bowl. Cover and refrigerate 20 minutes.

Remove leaves from bok choy stalks. Cut leaves into 2-inch pieces; cut stalks diagonally into ¼-inch slices (do not combine leaves and stalks). Remove strings from pea pods. Place pea pods in boiling water. Cover and cook 1 minute; drain. Immediately rinse in cold water; drain. Cut mushrooms into ½-inch slices. Cut green onions into 2-inch pieces; shred lengthwise into fine strips. Cover with iced water; let stand 10 minutes or until strips curl. Mix oyster sauce, 1 tablespoon cornstarch and the water.

Heat wok until very hot. Add 2 tablespoons vegetable oil; tilt wok to coat side. Add shrimp, gingerroot and garlic; stir-fry until shrimp are pink. Remove from wok.

Heat wok until very hot. Add 1 tablespoon vegetable oil; tilt wok to coat side. Add bok choy stalks, mushrooms and ½ teaspoon salt; stir-fry 1 minute. Add bok choy leaves and broth; heat to boiling. Stir in cornstarch mixture; cook and stir until thickened. Add shrimp and pea pods; cook and stir 1 minute or until shrimp are hot. Garnish with green onion curls. **4 servings**

PER SERVING: Calories 215; Protein 16 g; Carbohydrate 11 g; Fat 12 g; Cholesterol 105 mg; Sodium 1130 mg

Storing Shrimp

Keep frozen shrimp solidly frozen. Properly frozen, shrimp will keep for three months. When it's time to use the shrimp, thaw according to package directions.

Fresh, raw shrimp are best if cooked and served right after purchasing. Store in the refrigerator for one to two days. Rinse the shrimp in cold water and drain, then cover and refrigerate. Once cooked, store shrimp covered in the refrigerator for two to three days.

Shrimp with Fried Rice Stick Noodles

The rice stick noodles are sure to be a conversation piece.

1 pound fresh or frozen raw shrimp
1 teaspoon finely chopped gingerroot
½ teaspoon cornstarch
¼ teaspoon salt
¼ teaspoon sesame oil
Dash of white pepper
1 pound celery cabbage
3 large green onions
3 tablespoons cornstarch
3 tablespoons cold water
2 tablespoons dark soy sauce
Vegetable oil
4 ounces rice stick noodles
2 tablespoons vegetable oil
2 tablespoons vegetable oil
½ cup canned bamboo shoots, cut up
1 cup chicken broth

Peel shrimp. (If shrimp are frozen, do not thaw; peel under running cold water.) Make a shallow cut lengthwise down back of shrimp; wash out vein. Cut shrimp lengthwise into halves. Toss shrimp, gingerroot, ½ teaspoon cornstarch, the salt, sesame oil and white pepper. Cover and refrigerate 15 minutes. Cut celery cabbage into thin slices. Cut onions into 2-inch pieces. Mix 3 tablespoons cornstarch, the water and soy sauce.

Heat oil (1½ inches) in wok to 425°. Fry ¼ of the noodles at a time until puffed, turning once, about 5 seconds. Drain on paper towel. Wash and dry wok thoroughly.

Heat wok until 1 or 2 drops of water bubble and skitter when sprinkled in wok. Add 2 tablespoons vegetable oil; rotate. Add shrimp; stir-fry until shrimp is pink. Remove shrimp from wok.

Add 2 tablespoons oil to wok; rotate to coat side. Add celery cabbage and bamboo shoots; stir-fry 2 minutes. Stir in broth and shrimp; cover and heat to boiling. Stir in cornstarch mixture; cook and stir until thickened, about 10 seconds. Serve over noodles; garnish with onions.

5 servings

PER SERVING: Calories 290; Protein 12 g; Carbohydrate 11 g; Fat 22 g; Cholesterol 85 mg; Sodium 790 mg

Stir-fried Crabmeat with Celery Cabbage

Lobster with Chinese Vegetables

1½ pounds frozen lobster tails
1 package (6 ounces) frozen Chinese pea pods
3 medium stalks bok choy
2 tablespoons vegetable oil
2 cloves garlic, finely chopped
2 thin slices gingerroot, crushed
1 can (8½ ounces) water chestnuts, drained and thinly sliced
1 can (8½ ounces) bamboo shoots, drained
4 ounces mushrooms, sliced
1 can (10¾ ounces) condensed chicken broth
2 tablespoons cornstarch
2 tablespoons soy sauce
1 teaspoon salt
1 teaspoon sugar
¼ teaspoon white pepper
2 green onions, thinly sliced
Hot cooked rice

Cook lobster tails as directed on package; drain. Cut away thin undershell (covering meat of lobster) with kitchen scissors. Remove meat; cut into 1-inch pieces.

Rinse pea pods under running cold water to separate; drain. Separate leaves from bok choy stems; reserve leaves. Cut stems into ¼-inch slices. Heat oil in 12-inch skillet, Dutch oven or wok until hot. Cook and stir garlic and gingerroot over medium heat until brown. Add pea pods, bok choy stems, water chestnuts, bamboo shoots and mushrooms. Cook and stir over medium heat 2 minutes. Stir in ¾ cup of the broth; reduce heat. Cover and simmer 1 minute.

Mix remaining broth, the cornstarch, soy sauce, salt, sugar and white pepper; stir into vegetable mixture. Cook and stir until thickened, about 30 seconds. Tear bok choy leaves into bite-size pieces; add leaves and lobster to vegetable mixture. Heat until hot. Garnish with onions; serve with rice. **8 servings**

PER SERVING: Calories 250; Protein 11 g; Carbohydrate 40 g; Fat 5 g; Cholesterol 15 mg; Sodium 1250 mg

Stir-fried Crabmeat with Celery Cabbage

10 ounces frozen cooked crabmeat, thawed
½ pound celery cabbage
2 green onions (with tops)
1 tablespoon cornstarch
1 tablespoon water
1 teaspoon sugar
1 teaspoon roasted sesame oil
3 tablespoons vegetable oil
1 teaspoon finely chopped gingerroot
1 teaspoon finely chopped garlic
½ teaspoon salt
½ cup chicken broth

Drain crabmeat thoroughly; remove cartilage. Squeeze out excess moisture. Cut celery cabbage into 1-inch pieces. Cut green onions diagonally into 1-inch pieces. Mix cornstarch, water, sugar and sesame oil.

Heat wok until very hot. Add vegetable oil; tilt wok to coat side. Add gingerroot and garlic; stir-fry 30 seconds. Add celery cabbage and salt; stir-fry 1 minute.

Add broth; heat to boiling. Cover and cook 2 minutes over high heat. Stir in cornstarch mixture; cook and stir until thickened. Stir in crabmeat and green onions; cook and stir 1 minute or until crabmeat is hot. **4 servings**

PER SERVING: Calories 200; Protein 16 g; Carbohydrate 5 g; Fat 13 g; Cholesterol 70 mg; Sodium 570 mg

Zucchini and Potatoes in Curry Sauce (Recipe on page 81); Stir-fried Jicama with Black Mushrooms (Recipe on page 87)

4

Vegetables

Green Bean Stir-fry with Hoisin Sauce

Green beans take on an exotic, delicious flavor in this pleasing recipe.

1 pound green beans
2 tablespoons hoisin sauce
2 tablespoons dry sherry or chicken broth
1 teaspoon cornstarch
1 tablespoon vegetable oil
1 cup bean sprouts

Prepare green bean pieces as directed below. Mix hoison sauce, sherry and cornstarch.

Heat wok or 12-inch skillet until hot. Add oil and tilt wok to coat side. Add beans and bean sprouts. Stir-fry about 8 minutes or until beans are crisp-tender. Stir in hoisin sauce mixture. Cook and stir about 10 seconds or until thickened. **4 servings**

TO PREPARE: Wash beans; remove ends. Leave beans whole or cut crosswise into 1-inch pieces.

PER SERVING: Calories 90; Protein 2 g; Carbohydrate 11 g; Fat 4 g; Cholesterol 0 mg; Sodium 130 mg

Colorful Pepper Skillet

This dish is simply beautiful. Four brightly colored peppers, shiny with a touch of oil, are seasoned with cumin seed and the fresh flavor of cilantro.

1 teaspoon olive or vegetable oil
4 small bell peppers (green, purple, red and yellow), cut into strips
1 medium onion, thinly sliced
2 cloves garlic, finely chopped
1 tablespoon snipped fresh cilantro or 1 teaspoon dried cilantro leaves
1 teaspoon cumin seed

Heat oil in 10-inch nonstick skillet over medium-high heat until hot. Stir in remaining ingredients. Cook, stirring occasionally, until peppers are crisp-tender, 4 to 5 minutes. **6 servings**

PER SERVING: Calories 40; Protein 1 g; Carbohydrate 7 g; Fat 1 g; Cholesterol 0 mg; Sodium 200 mg

Skillet Peppers

3 medium bell peppers, cut into ¼-inch strips
1 medium onion, thinly sliced
¼ cup golden raisins
2 tablespoons olive oil or vegetable oil
2 tablespoons salted sunflower nuts
2 teaspoons lemon juice
½ teaspoon salt

Cook and stir bell peppers, onion and raisins in oil in 10-inch skillet over medium heat until bell peppers are tender, about 15 minutes. Stir in remaining ingredients. **4 servings**

PER SERVING: Calories 150 mg; Protein 2 g; Carbohydrate 15 g; Fat 9 g; Cholesterol 0 mg; Sodium 270 mg

Spicy Zucchini

Ground red pepper adds zest to this zucchini stir-fry. If you like very spicy foods, add a pinch more red pepper.

1 cup chicken broth
2 teaspoons cornstarch
3 cups ¼-inch slices zucchini (about 2 medium)
2 teaspoons paprika
1½ teaspoons chopped fresh or ½ teaspoon dried thyme leaves
1½ teaspoons chopped fresh or ½ teaspoon dried oregano leaves
⅛ teaspoon ground red pepper (cayenne)

Mix ¼ cup of the broth and the cornstarch in small bowl; reserve. Cook remaining broth and ingredients in 10-inch skillet over medium heat 7 to 10 minutes, stirring occasionally, until zucchini is tender. Stir in cornstarch mixture. Cook and stir 30 seconds or until thickened. **6 servings**

PER SERVING: Calories 20; Protein 1 g; Carbohydrate 4 g; Fat 0 g; Cholesterol 0 mg; Sodium 130 mg

Zucchini and Potatoes in Curry Sauce

Curry is an Indian flavoring, not tradition-ally Chinese, but Chinese cooks have been making their own version of curry power since 1900. Adding soy sauce makes the dish uniquely Far Eastern. It is important that curry powder be cooked (rather than added after cooking) to bring out the rich flavor of this spice mixture.

4 small zucchini (about 16 ounces)
2 medium potatoes (about 10 ounces)
1 medium tomato
1 small onion
¼ cup vegetable oil
2 teaspoons finely chopped garlic
1 tablespoon curry powder
2 teaspoons dark soy sauce
1 teaspoon sugar

Cut zucchini into ¾-inch pieces. Cut potatoes into ¾-inch pieces. Place tomato in boiling water; boil 30 seconds. Immediately rinse in cold water. Peel tomato; cut into ½-inch pieces. Cut onion into ½-inch pieces.

Heat wok until very hot. Add oil; tilt wok to coat side. Reduce heat to medium. Add potatoes; stir-fry about 4 minutes or until light brown. Remove potatoes from wok with slotted spoon; drain on paper towels.

Heat remaining oil in wok until hot. Add onion, garlic and curry powder; stir-fry until onion is tender. Add zucchini and tomato; stir-fry 2 minutes. Add potatoes, soy sauce and sugar; stir-fry 1 minute. **4 servings**

PER SERVING: Calories 220; Protein 2 g; Carbohy-drate 22 g; Fat 14 g; Cholesterol 0 mg; Sodium 180 mg

Stir-fried Zucchini and Jicama

1 medium zucchini (about ½ pound)
½ pound jicama
1 tablespoon vegetable oil
1 teaspoon sesame oil
1 tablespoon sesame seed
1 clove garlic, finely chopped
1 teaspoon salt

Prepare zucchini as directed below—except cut into julienne strips. Pare jicama and cut into juli-enne strips.

Heat wok or 12-inch skillet until 1 or 2 drops of water bubble and skitter when sprinkled in wok. Add vegetable oil and sesame oil. Rotate wok to coat side. Add sesame seed and garlic. Stir-fry 30 seconds. Add zucchini and jicama. Stir-fry 2 minutes. Stir in salt. **4 servings**

TO PREPARE: Wash zucchini; remove stem and blossom ends but do not pare. If zucchini are small, cut into halves. For larger zucchini, cut into ½ inch slices or cubes.

PER SERVING: Calories 75; Protein 1 g; Carbohy-drate 5 g; Fat 6 g; Cholesterol 0 mg; Sodium 580 mg

Vegetable Cutting Techniques

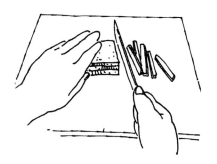

1. Dicing or Cubing: To dice means to cut into small pieces ½ inch or smaller. To cube is to cut into pieces larger than ½ inch. Cut vegetables into strips ½ inch wide for dicing or larger for cubing.

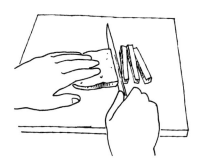

2. Stack or hold strips together and cut into pieces the same size as the width of the strips.

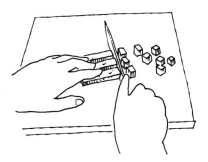

3. To shred: Cut vegetables into ⅛-inch slices. Stack slices; cut into thin strips.

Cucumber and Kale Stir-fry

Kale is a part of the cabbage family. Here, it's paired very nicely with cucumber.

2 medium cucumbers (about 1 pound)
1 tablespoon olive oil or vegetable oil
1 small onion, thinly sliced
1 clove garlic, finely chopped
2 cups torn kale pieces
2 teaspoons chopped fresh or ½ teaspoon dried basil leaves
¼ teaspoon salt
Dash of pepper

Pare cucumbers; cut lengthwise in half and remove seeds. Cut each half crosswise into ¼-inch slices. Heat oil in 12-inch skillet over medium heat. Cook cucumbers, onion and garlic in oil about 4 minutes, stirring occasionally, until cucumbers are crisp-tender. Stir in remaining ingredients. Cook and stir just until kale is wilted. **4 servings**

TO MICROWAVE: Omit oil. Prepare cucumbers as directed—except place cucumbers, onion, garlic, basil, salt and pepper in 2-quart microwavable casserole. Cover tightly and microwave on high 3 to 4 minutes or until cucumbers are crisp-tender. Stir in kale. Cover tightly and microwave on high 1 to 2 minutes longer or just until kale is wilted.

PER SERVING: Calories 65; Protein 2 g; Carbohydrate 8 g; Fat 4 g; Cholesterol 0 mg; Sodium 150 mg

Mixed Vegetables

1 tablespoon chicken bouillon granules
½ cup water
1 tablespoon cornstarch
1 tablespoon cold water
1 tablespoon soy sauce
8 ounces bean sprouts
2 tablespoons vegetable oil
1 medium onion, thinly sliced
2 large cloves garlic, finely chopped
1 teaspoon finely chopped gingerroot
4 medium stalks celery, cut into ¼-inch slices (about 2 cups)
1 package (10 ounces) frozen green peas
8 ounces mushrooms, cut into ¼-inch slices (about 3 cups)

Mix bouillon granules in ½ cup water. Dissolve cornstarch in 1 tablespoon water and the soy sauce.

Rinse bean sprouts under running cold water; drain. Heat wok or 12-inch skillet over medium-high heat until 1 or 2 drops water bubble and skitter when sprinkled in wok. Add oil; rotate wok to coat side. Add onion, garlic and gingerroot; stir-fry until garlic is light brown. Add celery and peas; stir-fry 3 minutes. Add mushrooms and bean sprouts; stir-fry 1 minute. Stir in bouillon mixture; heat to boiling. Stir in cornstarch mixture; cook and stir until thickened, about 10 seconds. **8 servings**

PER SERVING: Calories 140; Protein 7 g; Carbohydrate 14 g; Fat 6 g; Cholesterol 0 mg; Sodium 660 mg

Cucumber and Tomato Skillet

2 medium cucumbers (about 1 pound)
2 tablespoons margarine or butter
1 medium onion, sliced and separated into rings
2 medium tomatoes, cut into wedges
½ teaspoon salt
Dash of pepper
1 tablespoon chopped fresh or 1 teaspoon dried dill weed

Prepare cucumbers as directed below—except cut into 1-inch pieces. Heat margarine in 12-inch skillet over medium heat. Cook cucumbers and onion in margarine about 5 minutes, stirring occasionally, until cucumbers are crisp-tender. Stir in tomatoes. Sprinkle with salt and pepper. Cook, stirring occasionally, just until tomatoes are hot. Sprinkle with dill. **6 servings**

TO PREPARE: Wash cucumbers; pare if desired and seed if desired. Cut into ½-inch slices or ½-inch pieces.

PER SERVING: Calories 55; Protein 1 g; Carbohydrate 5 g; Fat 4 g; Cholesterol 0 mg; Sodium 230 mg

Bok Choy with Soy Sauce

1 cup tomato juice
2 cloves garlic, finely chopped (about 1 teaspoon)
1 teaspoon finely chopped gingerroot
4 cups chopped bok choy (about ⅓ medium head)
1 cup chopped mushrooms (about 4 ounces)
½ cup chopped yellow bell pepper (about 1 small)
¼ cup chopped green onions (2 to 3 medium)
2 tablespoons chopped fresh cilantro leaves
2 tablespoons lime juice
1 teaspoon reduced-sodium soy sauce

Mix ½ cup of the tomato juice, the garlic and gingerroot in 10-inch skillet. Cook over medium heat 2 minutes. Stir in remaining tomato juice, the bok choy, mushrooms, bell pepper and onions. Cook 3 minutes, stirring occasionally, until bok choy leaves are wilted. Stir in remaining ingredients. **6 servings**

PER SERVING: Calories 25; Protein 1 g; Carbohydrate 5 g; Fat 0 g; Cholesterol 0 mg; Sodium 215 mg

Bok Choy Stir-fry

The pale, Oriental bok choy has become nearly a staple in American markets. Bok choy leaves cook more rapidly than the stems, so they are added for only a brief toss in the skillet.

1½ pounds bok choy
1 tablespoon cornstarch
2 tablespoons soy sauce
1 tablespoon vegetable oil
1 tablespoon reduced-calorie margarine
2 teaspoons finely chopped gingerroot
1 clove garlic, finely chopped
2 tablespoons water

Separate bok choy leaves from stems. Cut leaves into ½-inch strips; cut stems into ¼-inch slices. Mix cornstarch and soy sauce. Heat oil and margarine in 12-inch skillet over medium-high heat until margarine is melted. Add gingerroot and garlic; stir-fry until garlic is light brown. Add bok choy stems; stir-fry 2 minutes. Add water; cover and cook until stems are crisp-tender, about 2 minutes. Stir in cornstarch mixture and bok choy leaves; stir-fry until leaves are wilted, 1 to 2 minutes. **6 servings**

PER SERVING: Calories 60; Protein 2 g; Carbohydrate 4 g; Fat 4 g; Cholesterol 0 mg; Sodium 430 mg

Slicing Celery and Bok Choy

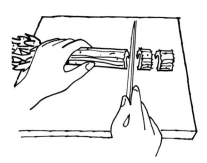

1. Cut straight across the widest end of the stalk.

2. As it becomes narrower, cut across the stalk at an angle.

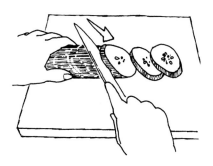

3. Diagonal Slicing. Keep the blade angle of a very sharp knife almost parallel to the cutting surface to slice on the diagonal.

Lemon-Pepper Vegetables

1 cup ¼-inch yellow squash slices (about 1 medium)
1 small red bell pepper, cut into ¼-inch strips
⅓ cup diagonally cut celery slices (about 1 small stalk)
⅓ cup 1-inch green onion pieces, with tops (about 3)
1 teaspoon vegetable oil
1 tablespoon lemon juice
¼ teaspoon lemon pepper
4 ounces Chinese pea pods*

Cook and stir squash, bell pepper, celery and onions in oil in 10-inch nonstick skillet over medium-high heat until pepper is crisp-tender, about 2 minutes. Stir in remaining ingredients; cook and stir until pea pods are hot, about 1 minute longer. **6 servings**

1 package (6 ounces) frozen pea pods, thawed, can be substituted for pea pods.

MICROWAVE DIRECTIONS: Mix all ingredients except pea pods in 1½-quart microwavable casserole. Cover tightly and microwave on high 3 minutes. Stir in pea pods. Cover and microwave until pea pods are hot, 1 to 3 minutes longer.

PER SERVING: Calories 35; Protein 2 g; Carbohydrate 5 g; Fat 1 g; Cholesterol 0 mg; Sodium 10 mg

Stir-fried Eggplant and Peppers

Stir-fried Eggplant and Peppers

1 medium eggplant
1 green bell pepper
1 red bell pepper
8 medium mushrooms
2 tablespoons oyster sauce
1 tablespoon sugar
3 tablespoons vegetable oil
2 teaspoons finely chopped garlic
1 teaspoon finely chopped gingerroot
1 teaspoon sesame oil

Pare eggplant if desired; cut into fourths and remove seeds. Cut into 2 × ¾ × ¼-inch strips. Cover with cold water; let stand 30 minutes. Drain; pat dry with paper towels. Cut bell peppers into ¼-inch strips. Cut mushrooms into ½-inch slices. Mix oyster sauce and sugar.

Heat wok until hot. Add vegetable oil; tilt wok to coat side. Add eggplant, garlic and gingerroot; stir-fry 1 minute. Add bell peppers and mushrooms; stir-fry 2 minutes. Add oyster sauce mixture and sesame oil; cook and stir 1 minute.   **4 servings**

PER SERVING: Calories 190; Protein 3 g; Carbohydrate 18 g; Fat 12 g; Cholesterol 0 mg; Sodium 350 mg

Triple Mushroom Stir-fry

Dried black mushrooms are also known as Chinese dried mushrooms.

8 medium dried black mushrooms
2 teaspoons vegetable oil
3 cups ¼-inch mushroom slices (about 8 ounces)
1 jar (7 ounces) enoki mushrooms, drained
1 clove garlic, finely chopped
½ cup 1-inch green onion pieces, with tops (about 3)

Soak black mushrooms in warm water to cover until soft, about 30 minutes; drain. Remove and discard stems; slice caps.

Heat oil in wok or 10-inch nonstick skillet over medium-high heat until hot. Add mushrooms and garlic; stir-fry 1 minute. Add onions; stir-fry 1 minute longer.   **4 servings**

PER SERVING: Calories 45; Protein 2 g; Carbohydrate 4 g; Fat 3 g; Cholesterol 0 mg; Sodium 110 mg

Stir-fried Jicama with Black Mushrooms

8 medium dried black mushrooms
4 shallots
3 stalks celery
8 ounces jicama
3 tablespoons vegetable oil
¼ teaspoon salt
¼ cup chicken broth
¼ teaspoon sugar

Soak mushrooms in hot water 20 minutes or until soft; drain. Rinse in warm water; drain. Squeeze out excess moisture. Remove and discard stems; cut caps into ¼-inch slices. Cut shallots into fourths. Cut celery diagonally into ¼-inch slices. Pare jicama and cut into 2-inch-wide pieces; cut into ¼-inch slices.

Heat wok until very hot. Add oil; tilt wok to coat side. Add mushrooms, shallots, celery and salt; stir-fry 1 minute. Add broth and sugar; cook and stir 1 minute or until all moisture has evaporated. Add jicama; cook and stir 1 minute.

4 servings

PER SERVING: Calories 145; Protein 2 g; Carbohydrate 9 g; Fat 11 g; Cholesterol 0 mg; Sodium 210 mg

Stir-fried Bok Choy with Tofu

Stir-fried Bok Choy with Tofu

Tofu, a culinary chameleon, takes on the exotic flavor of oyster sauce and shallots here. Dusting the tofu cubes with cornstarch makes them easier to handle and produces a firm, crisp exterior. If not using a wok, use a saucepan or skillet with high sides. Tofu is very moist, and oil may splatter.

8 large stalks bok choy
1 pound firm tofu
2 tablespoons cornstarch
3 shallots
2 tablespoons vegetable oil
2 tablespoons oyster sauce
2 tablespoons vegetable oil
½ teaspoon salt

Remove leaves from bok choy stems. Cut leaves into 2-inch pieces; cut stems diagonally into ¼-inch slices (do not combine leaves and stems). Cut tofu into 1 × 1 × 1¼-inch pieces. Coat tofu with cornstarch. Cut shallots into thin slices.

Heat wok until very hot. Add 2 tablespoons vegetable oil; tilt wok to coat side. Add tofu; fry 2 pieces at a time 1 minute, turning once. Repeat with remaining tofu; return all tofu to wok. Add oyster sauce; toss until tofu is evenly coated. Remove tofu from wok.

Heat wok until very hot. Add 2 tablespoons vegetable oil; tilt wok to coat side. Add shallots; stir-fry 30 seconds. Add bok choy stems and salt; stir-fry 1 minute. Add tofu and bok choy leaves; cover and cook 1 minute over high heat.

4 servings

PER SERVING: Calories 355; Protein 21 g; Carbohydrate 12 g; Fat 25 g; Cholesterol 0 mg; Sodium 660 mg

Subgum Tofu

1 pound tofu
8 ounces bok choy (about 4 large stalks)
4 ounces pea pods
1 medium red bell pepper
2 green onions (with tops)
2 tablespoons cornstarch
2 tablespoons cold water
3 tablespoons vegetable oil
2 tablespoons vegetable oil
1 can (13 ounces) whole straw mushrooms, drained
½ cup sliced canned water chestnuts
½ cup chicken broth
¼ cup oyster sauce

Cut tofu into pieces, 1 × 1 × ¼ inch. Cut bok choy (with leaves) diagonally into ¼-inch slices. Remove strings from pea pods. Place pea pods in boiling water. Cover and cook 1 minute; drain. Immediately rinse under running cold water; drain. Cut bell pepper into ½-inch strips. Cut onions into 2-inch pieces. Mix cornstarch and water.

Heat wok until 1 or 2 drops of water bubble and skitter when sprinkled in wok. Add 3 tablespoons oil; rotate wok to coat side. Add tofu; cook, stirring carefully, 2 minutes. Remove tofu from wok.

Add 2 tablespoons oil to wok; rotate to coat side. Add bok choy; stir-fry 1 minute. Add mushrooms and water chestnuts; stir-fry 1 minute. Stir in chicken broth and oyster sauce; heat to boiling. Stir in cornstarch mixture; cook and stir until thickened. Stir in tofu, bell pepper, green onions and pea pods. **5 servings**

PER SERVING: Calories 270; Protein 12 g; Carbohydrate 15 g; Fat 18 g; Cholesterol 0 mg; Sodium 880 mg

Gingered Spinach

Wash fresh spinach very thoroughly in cold water to rid it completely of sand.

2 teaspoons finely chopped gingerroot
2 teaspoons peanut oil or vegetable oil
¼ teaspoon sesame oil
1 teaspoon soy sauce
½ pound fresh spinach
1 cup julienne strips jicama (about 4 ounces)
2 teaspoons toasted sesame seed

Cook and stir gingerroot in peanut and sesame oils in 10-inch nonstick skillet over medium-high heat. Stir in soy sauce and half of the spinach. Cook and stir until spinach begins to wilt. Stir in remaining spinach and the jicama. Cook and stir until spinach is wilted and jicama is hot, about 2 minutes longer. Sprinkle with sesame seed. **4 servings**

PER SERVING: Calories 80; Protein 2 g; Carbohydrate 11 g; Fat 3 g; Cholesterol 0 mg; Sodium 130 mg

Mixed Sprouts and Broccoli

Stir-frying in broth instead of oil cuts calories, but not flavor. Any leftovers can become a refreshing cold salad, or be stirred into a vegetable-pasta dish.

½ cup bean sprouts
½ cup chopped green onions (about 5 medium)
⅓ cup chicken broth
2½ cups cooked broccoli flowerets (about 1 pound)
2 tablespoons lime juice
2 teaspoons reduced-sodium soy sauce
1 teaspoon sesame oil
¼ cup alfalfa sprouts

Cook bean sprouts, onions and broth in 10-inch skillet over medium heat 3 minutes or until bean sprouts are wilted. Stir in broccoli, lime juice and soy sauce. Cook, stirring frequently, until broccoli is heated through. Stir in sesame oil and alfalfa sprouts. **6 servings**

PER SERVING: Calories 35; Protein 2 g; Carbohydrate 4 g; Fat 1 g; Cholesterol 0 mg; Sodium 135 mg

Stir-fried Broccoli and Carrots

2 teaspoons finely chopped gingerroot
1 clove garlic, finely chopped
1½ cups small broccoli flowerets
1 cup thinly sliced carrots (about 2 medium)
1 small onion, sliced and separated into rings
¾ cup chicken broth
¼ teaspoon salt
1 tablespoon cornstarch
1 tablespoon cold water
1 can (8 ounces) sliced water chestnuts, drained
1 cup sliced mushrooms (about 3 ounces)
2 tablespoons oyster sauce

Spray wok or 12-inch skillet with nonstick cooking spray; heat until hot. Add gingerroot and garlic; stir-fry about 1 minute or until light brown. Add broccoli, carrots and onion; stir-fry 1 minute. Stir in broth and salt; cover and cook about 3 minutes or until carrots are crisp-tender. Mix cornstarch and cold water; stir into vegetable mixture. Cook and stir about 10 seconds or until thickened. Add water chestnuts, mushrooms and oyster sauce; cook and stir 30 seconds. **4 servings**

PER SERVING: Calories 95; Protein 3 g; Carbohydrate 18 g; Fat 1 g; Cholesterol 0 mg; Sodium 560 mg

Saucy Okra and Pepper

The cornmeal is very versatile here. First, it absorbs the natural thickener released when the okra is cooked, and helps to brown the okra. When the broth is added, it dissolves and helps create a tasty sauce.

⅓ **cup stone-ground or degerminated cornmeal**
½ **teaspoon paprika**
¼ **teaspoon salt**
⅛ **teaspoon pepper**
2½ **cups sliced fresh or 1 package (10 ounces) frozen cut okra, thawed**
1 **cup chopped red bell pepper (about 1 medium)**
2 **tablespoons chopped green onions**
1 **cup chicken broth**

Spray 10-inch nonstick skillet with nonstick cooking spray. Mix cornmeal, paprika, salt and pepper. Coat okra with cornmeal mixture. Heat skillet until hot. Cook okra in skillet over medium heat 7 to 10 minutes or until brown on all sides. Stir in remaining ingredients. Cook 3 minutes, stirring constantly, until sauce thickens.

6 servings

PER SERVING: Calories 60; Protein 2 g; Carbohydrate 11 g; Fat 1 g; Cholesterol 0 mg; Sodium 220 mg

Sweet-and-Sour Cabbage

1 **medium head cabbage (about 1 pound)**
4 **shallots**
1 **tablespoon cornstarch**
1 **tablespoon water**
3 **tablespoons vegetable oil**
¼ **cup ketchup**
3 **tablespoons sugar**
1 **teaspoon salt**
1 **teaspoon red pepper sauce**
½ **cup chicken broth**

Cut cabbage into 1½-inch pieces. Cut shallots into fourths. Mix cornstarch and water.

Heat wok until very hot. Add oil; tilt wok to coat side. Add cabbage; stir-fry 1 minute. Add shallots, ketchup, sugar, salt and pepper sauce; stir-fry 1 minute. Add broth; heat to boiling. Stir in cornstarch mixture; cook and stir 10 seconds or until thickened.

4 servings

PER SERVING: Calories 220; Protein 3 g; Carbohydrate 27 g; Fat 11 g; Cholesterol 0 mg; Sodium 860 mg

Straw Mushrooms with Tofu

8 ounces tofu
4 ounces pea pods
2 green onions (with tops)
1 tablespoon cornstarch
1 tablespoon cold water
3 tablespoons vegetable oil
4 thin slices gingerroot
1 can (13 ounces) whole straw mushrooms, drained
¼ teaspoon salt
¼ cup chicken broth
2 tablespoons oyster sauce or 1 tablespoon soy sauce

Cut tofu into halves; cut each half into ¼-inch slices. Remove strings from pea pods. Place pea pods in boiling water. Cover and cook 1 minute; drain. Immediately rinse under running cold water; drain. Cut onions into 2-inch pieces. Mix cornstarch and water.

Heat wok until 1 or 2 drops of water bubble and skitter when sprinkled in wok. Add oil; rotate wok to coat side. Add gingerroot; stir-fry until brown. Remove and discard gingerroot. Add tofu; cook 20 seconds. Turn tofu carefully; cook 20 seconds longer. Add mushrooms and salt; stir-fry 1 minute (do not break tofu). Stir in chicken broth and oyster sauce; heat to boiling. Stir in cornstarch mixture; cook and stir until thickened, about 10 seconds. Add pea pods and onions; cook and stir 30 seconds. **4 servings**

PER SERVING: Calories 190; Protein 8 g; Carbohydrate 10 g; Fat 13 g; Cholesterol 0 mg; Sodium 810 mg

Stir-fried Rice Noodles with Vegetables

In this recipe, the rice noodles are boiled briefly before being stir-fried with soy sauce and then served topped with a variety of Chinese vegetables. Use a nonstick skillet if you don't have a wok, and toss the noodles continuously so they don't overcook.

6 medium dried black mushrooms
1 medium carrot
4 ounces Chinese pea pods
3 large stalks bok choy
3 green onions (with tops)
1 cup sliced canned bamboo shoots
1 tablespoon cornstarch
1 tablespoon water
8 ounces rice stick noodles
2 quarts water
2 tablespoons vegetable oil
2 teaspoons soy sauce
3 tablespoons vegetable oil
¾ cup chicken broth

Soak mushrooms in hot water 20 minutes or until soft; drain. Rinse in warm water; drain. Squeeze out excess moisture. Remove and discard stems; cut caps into thin strips.

Cut carrot into 2-inch pieces. Cut pieces lengthwise into ⅛-inch slices. Cut slices lengthwise into ⅛-inch strips. Place carrots in boiling water. Heat to boiling; drain. Immediately rinse in cold water. Remove strings from pea pods. Place pea pods in boiling water. Cover and cook 1 minute; drain. Immediately rinse in cold water; drain. Cut each pea pod lengthwise into 3 or 4 strips.

Remove leaves from bok choy stems. Cut leaves into 2-inch pieces; cut stems diagonally into ¼-inch slices (do not combine leaves and stems). Cut green onions diagonally into

1½-inch pieces. Cut bamboo shoots lengthwise into thin strips. Mix cornstarch and 1 tablespoon water.

Pull noodles apart. Heat 2 quarts water to boiling; stir in noodles. Cook uncovered 1 minute; drain. Rinse in cold water; drain.

Heat wok until very hot. Add 2 tablespoons oil; tilt wok to coat side. Add noodles; stir-fry 2 minutes or until tender. Stir in soy sauce. Remove noodles from wok. Place on heatproof platter; keep warm in 300° oven.

Heat wok until very hot. Add 3 tablespoons oil; tilt wok to coat side. Add mushrooms, bok choy stems and bamboo shoots; stir-fry 1 minute. Add broth; heat to boiling. Stir in cornstarch mixture; cook and stir until thickened. Stir in carrot, pea pods, bok choy leaves and green onions; heat to boiling. Pour vegetable mixture over noodles. **4 servings**

PER SERVING: Calories 340; Protein 5 g; Carbohydrate 40 g; Fat 18 g; Cholesterol 0 mg; Sodium 350 mg

Blanching Vegetables

Blanching is quick, partial cooking to preserve the texture, color and flavor of vegetables, and it can make your stir-fries even quicker. To blanch, prepare vegetables according to the recipe. Place in a wire strainer and lower into boiling water; cover. Blanch tender vegetables like pea pods and green beans about 30 seconds or just until water returns to a boil. Blanch tougher vegetables like broccoli stems about two minutes. Rinse vegetables under running cold water or immediately plunge them into cold water to cool. Remove from water; drain. Vegetables are now ready to be used in your recipe.

White and Wild Rice Stir-fry

⅓ **cup uncooked regular long grain rice**
⅓ **cup uncooked wild rice**
¾ **cup thinly sliced red onion (about 1 small)**
2 **cloves garlic, finely chopped (about 1 teaspoon)**
¾ **cup chicken broth**
½ **cup chopped yellow bell pepper (about 1 small)**
¼ **cup raisins**
¼ **cup chopped dried apricots**
¼ **teaspoon salt**
¼ **teaspoon pepper**
¼ **cup chopped fresh parsley**
2 **tablespoons red wine vinegar**
1 **teaspoon olive oil or vegetable oil**

Prepare regular rice as directed on package—except omit salt. Prepare wild rice as directed on package—except omit salt. Cook onion, garlic and broth in 10-inch skillet over medium-high heat 5 to 6 minutes, stirring occasionally, until liquid has almost evaporated. Stir in regular rice, wild rice, bell pepper, raisins, apricots, salt and pepper. Cook over medium heat 2 minutes; stirring constantly, until heated through. Stir in parsley, vinegar and oil. **6 servings**

PER SERVING: Calories 130; Protein 3 g; Carbohydrate 27 g; Fat 1 g; Cholesterol 0 mg; Sodium 190 mg

METRIC CONVERSION GUIDE

U.S. UNITS	CANADIAN METRIC	AUSTRALIAN METRIC
Volume		
1/4 teaspoon	1 mL	1 ml
1/2 teaspoon	2 mL	2 ml
1 teaspoon	5 mL	5 ml
1 tablespoon	15 mL	20 ml
1/4 cup	50 mL	60 ml
1/3 cup	75 mL	80 ml
1/2 cup	125 mL	125 ml
2/3 cup	150 mL	170 ml
3/4 cup	175 mL	190 ml
1 cup	250 mL	250 ml
1 quart	1 liter	1 liter
1 1/2 quarts	1.5 liter	1.5 liter
2 quarts	2 liters	2 liters
2 1/2 quarts	2.5 liters	2.5 liters
3 quarts	3 liters	3 liters
4 quarts	4 liters	4 liters
Weight		
1 ounce	30 grams	30 grams
2 ounces	55 grams	60 grams
3 ounces	85 grams	90 grams
4 ounces (1/4 pound)	115 grams	125 grams
8 ounces (1/2 pound)	225 grams	225 grams
16 ounces (1 pound)	455 grams	500 grams
1 pound	455 grams	1/2 kilogram

Measurements		Temperatures	
Inches	Centimeters	Fahrenheit	Celsius
1	2.5	32°	0°
2	5.0	212°	100°
3	7.5	250°	120°
4	10.0	275°	140°
5	12.5	300°	150°
6	15.0	325°	160°
7	17.5	350°	180°
8	20.5	375°	190°
9	23.0	400°	200°
10	25.5	425°	220°
11	28.0	450°	230°
12	30.5	475°	240°
13	33.0	500°	260°
14	35.5		
15	38.0		

NOTE
The recipes in this cookbook have not been developed or tested using metric measures. When converting recipes to metric, some variations in quality may be noted.

Index

Page numbers in *italics* indicate photographs.